Dedication

We are bound to our ancestors and to   we want to be or not. What matters is what we make of what we are. Our ancestors have invented, we can at least innovate. We rarely know who our ancestors were. Who can even remember the names of their great-grandparents? They have vanished into the dim and distant past.

In Honour of the Late Mr Benny Govender

22 /11/1935 to 03/10/2004

CHAPTER 1

Seeing a bright light at the end of a dark tunnel is quite common, as is leaving one's body and floating above it or even journeying off into space. Meeting loved ones, living or dead, as well as other beings such as angels, or even major figures such as Moses or Jesus, is frequently reported. Subjects feel bathed in unconditional love and deeply connected to the cosmos.

Sometimes subjects are asked, after seeing a review of their lifetime memories, what efforts they made during their lives to grow in wisdom and love. Subjects want to remain in this realm but are told they must return to their bodies.

Sheffield in England 11th March 1864

On the night before the flood, Sarah had a very peculiar dream. She dreamt that she was in a flood and that she had a very narrow bridge to cross, but with great difficulty, she managed to get across. It was the dream that would consequently save her. The clock stopped at two minutes past twelve, and that, as the clock was right to the minute, that was the time of the flood.

"The river beneath me began to swell, water cascading over the rocks. Clouds began to rumble and darken. Steadily building into a thunderous deluge, icy sheets of rain began to pout mercilessly from the ever-darkening sky, making the unpaved bridge awash with mud and obscuring my vision. Suddenly a fork of lightning, brilliant and buzzing with magnificent electricity, flashed majestically through the groaning mountain of clouds. Whistling and shrieking, the wind raged through the night, like an angered bear.

Thunder rippled, the noise enveloped the river and its surroundings, and the trees nearby were sleek with torrents of rain cold rainwater. The wind demanded to be heard. The lightning fought to be seen. The rain lived to soak my clothes. The storm had broken. "

Extremely near to the house of Henry Whistles at Hill Bridge House, was the Mason's Arms public house kept by William Pickering.

The house was almost destroyed, the interior exposed, and all the furniture swept away. In the house at the time of the floor, beside Pickering himself, were his wife, his sister, a lodger, and a little girl, a niece, eight years of age. All were drowned except the little girl. She slept by herself in a bed in a chamber on the top story of the house, higher than the line where the water rose. When the neighbours went to the house on the morning after the flood, they found that nearly everything had been swept away but on going to the upper chamber they were astonished to find the little girl in bed and fast asleep. They woke her and took her to a place of safety. The house was swept away except a little corner on which the girl's bed stood. Upon being questioned she said -" I heard a noise in the middle of the night. I thought the gas was blowing up downstairs. I heard my uncle go downstairs and thought if he was going to see if the gas had blown up. I then heard my aunt go down and call out for help. Her sister went to her, and I then heard them both cry out for help. I heard nothing more and went to sleep soon afterward.'

I AM DEAD - HE KILLED ME

Please tell me what happened that day……June 1905, Port of Madras, India

India

The district of Chingleput supplied nearly 10% of the Madras passengers to Natal.

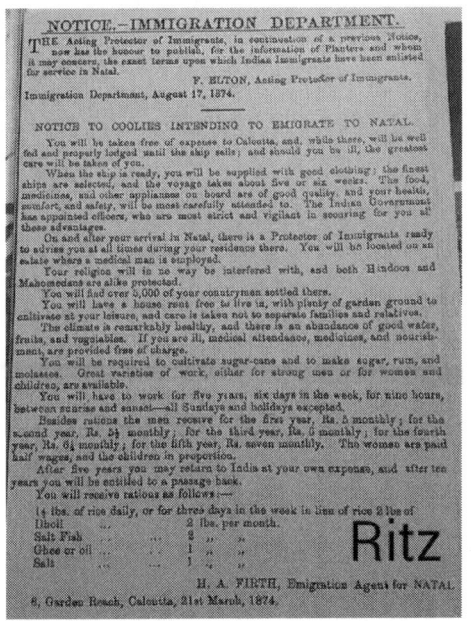

Great grandfather was from the city of Madras Chingleput.

Chingleput district The town was called Maduratakum and the village of Rajampoliam

They came on boats searching for hope in a new land. Unaware of what lay ahead of them

They took their chances, even if it meant that they were treated like slaves

Signing documents they often didn't understand They came in their numbers, ready for work

Ploughing the cane fields and working as servants They were determined to succeed, as they wanted a better life for their children. We thank our forefathers for their sacrifices and their ambition to succeed and fight for our rights. Thank you for the fond memories. A temple that still stands today in Tinley Manor was built by our great grandfather Ellappa Govender.

We should never forget our heritage, never be ashamed of who we are, and like our forefathers - our families should always be a priority. History does not merely refer to the past, on the contrary, the great force of history comes from the fact that we carry it within us, are unconsciously controlled by it in so many ways and it is literally present in all we do.

"We inherit from our ancestor's gifts so often taken for granted.

Each of us contains within this inheritance of soul. We are links between the ages, containing past and present expectations, sacred memories, and future promise."

When we know about our ancestors, when we sense them as living and as supporting us, then we feel connected to the genetic life-stream, and we draw strength and nourishment from this.

The majority of Indian South Africans are the descendants of indentured workers brought to Natal between 1860 and 1911 to develop the sugar industry in the province of Natal. The first recorded reference to Natal Colonists' demand for indentured labour appears in a report in the Durban Observer on 17th October 1851 at a meeting of citizens held at the Durban Government school hall where a motion calling for the introduction of indentured labour was passed. However, it must be noted that the first Indians, four in number, had been brought to Natal in 1849.

Jan Van Riebeek had as early as the 1650s brought Indians as slaves to South Africa. During the 17th and 18th centuries, over 50% of all slaves at the Cape were Indian from Bengal and South India.

The Natal Government had to revise its legislation before the introduction of Indian workers in the colony. The Law stipulated that a minimum number of women in every shipload and ship often waited for days before they could depart for Natal as it did not have the requisite 25% of its passenger quota.

The immigrants signed no contract but merely put their mark on a written statement which served to confirm that the person had agreed to serve his/her employer to whom they were to be allotted to by the Natal Government and that they understood that the wages for the first year were to be 10 shillings, 11 shillings for the second year and 12 shillings for the third year.

The Indian population of South Africa owes its presence in the country to the labour problems experienced by pioneer sugar-cane farmers in Natal. For the cultivation and reaping of sugar cane and the manufacture of sugar, a certain type of labour was needed and Indian coolies (laborers) were eminently suited for this purpose. The SS Truro left Madras on 13.10.1860 and dropped anchor at Port Natal (Durban) on 16.11.1860.

It carried a consignment of 340 Labourers - 197 men, 89 women, and 54 children. These people hailed from all parts of Southern and Eastern India and different factors motivated them. For the majority, it was a case of escaping from conditions of extreme poverty, while others were spurred by ambition and adventure. The majority were Hindus belonging to various caste systems.

The people in this group were not so much field workers like mechanics, domestics, gardeners, others qualified for various trades, barbers, carpenters, accountants, nurses, and maids. It was more of a heterogeneous assortment than a supply of laborers for the sugar cane plantations. This list disproves the statement that all indentured laborers were recruited from the untouchables who were living in semi-starvation conditions in India.

The immigrant laborers came from the cultivating ranks of the great river plains of India. Their life was anchored by a satisfying wealth of symbolism and pageantry which, proceeding under the guise of religious dogmas and precepts, kept them united and provided the strength of character in the face of formidable assaults made on their beliefs by those who regarded Hinduism as pagan and heathen and full of superstition. A remarkable scene was the landing of the first batch of indentured laborers. The spectators present had been led to expect a group of dried-up, vapid and sleepy-looking people. They were disappointed when the swarthy hordes came out of the boat's hold, laughing, jabbering, and sharing with a satisfied expression of self-complacency on their faces.

The majority of those who arrived in this country could neither read nor write but some knowledge of the treasure-house of their religion, culture, and traditions. They had learned much about their religion by word of mouth and they passed this on to their children in the same oral tradition. They also brought with them the caste system, their religious practices, rituals, and dogmas, kept them alive, and handed them to succeeding generations. Some mendicant bards were literate and knew portions of the great epics.

A temple that still stands today in Tinley Manor was built by our great grandfather Ellappa and Mr. Waterkotri Moonsamy.

'This vibrant example of the community-built architecture dates to 1913 and is home to more than 150 loosely interpreted and idiosyncratically rendered sculptures of deities, all produced under the leadership of local sculptor Ellapa Govender, who also helped to design and build the temple. The entire community contributed to making the bricks and mixing and casting the concrete, and the sense of love and devotion embedded into the site is still clearly evident today. The site is one of the finest examples of folk architecture in South Africa by Ellappa Govender.'

The idea of building a temple in 1913 originated from Perumal Naicker.

Those responsible for designing and building the temple were Ellappa Govender, Waterkotri Munsamy, and Patchappa Govender. While the cooperation of the entire community was enlisted in making bricks, mixing concrete, etc, those who played a vital role in its construction were V Reddy, C Reddy, L Moonsamy, M Mundhree, G Govender, P Govender, and M Govender.

Our ancestors who changed the world did so through new ideas which came to them.

Son of a Sepoy, the late Mr. Perumal Naicker was born about 1864 at Coornthur in the North Arcot District. Having completed fine academic courses in Tamil, Telugu, Malayalam, and Sanskrit, the late

Mr. Perumal Naicker first tried his hand at teaching but soon left for Natal. To seek fresh pastures and relatives who had emigrated earlier.

Upon his arrival in Natal, he had to serve Sir J.L. Huletts and Sons as a farm labourer on the sugar fields at Tinley Manor. The onerous task of plying labour in this blazing heat was beyond the reverend gentleman. To his good fortune, his immediate seniors recognized his cultural background and deemed it fit to employ him in furtherance of religious aspects and cultural aspects in the context of the Indian population at Tinley Manor.

The first task that the late Mr. Perumal Naicker accomplished was the building of the Siva Soobramoniar Temple which is a landmark on the North Coast.

The grand old man needed no urging to continue his contribution towards his society at Tinley Manor. He decided to start a school and in his estimation an English School was indispensable. Armed with his stringed instrument and garbed in ochre, the old man went to Durban where he began to interview people to find a teacher. He found Mr. K.T. Subban and came with him to Tinley Manor to start a school. So began the Tinley Manor State Aided Indian School.

In 1937, the late Mr. Perumal Naicker erected a Venkata Perumal Temple in Groutville. The temple stands on the main road to Stanger.

His daughter-in-law, Mrs. Jaganathan P Naicker, who now lives at Groutville receives those old associates of the late Mr. Perumal Naicker with all due respect.

The late Mr. Perumal Naicker is no more, the memory of his being may fade away but the product of his endeavours will fill many a heart with joy.

Tinley Manor Shiva Temple

Although it has been a particularly difficult task to establish who exactly was responsible for building the various temples around the country., it soon became evident that several itinerant temple builders moved from village to village to erect these buildings. None of them, as far as we know, had any formal training in this field, although they soon, became completely competent and professional in their newfound calling. Each one had his particular approach and this is useful in the identification of the various builders. How wonderful it is then to find a temple accomplished with little grandeur, yet built for a community totally by the community itself.

There is a sense of love and devotion built into the temple at Tinley Manor which is clearly evident to the visitor. Apparently, the idea of the Temple was Perumal Naicker's. He, together with a certain Boiler Moonsamy, travelled throughout Natal to collect funds. **Ellappa Govender** and Waterkotri Munsamy (known by that name as he worked at the nearby Waterson Estate), together with **Patachappa Govender**, designed and built the temple over two years from 1913 to 1914. The whole community was inspanned to make bricks, mix cement and cast concrete and sand, but it is especially Vegnal Reddy, Challappa Reddy, Lawer Moonsamy, Muruva Mundhee, and the following Govender's; Gopal, Patachappa, Moonsamy, (known as Banana and Poonappa,) who are today remembered for their stout effort during the construction period. Under the leadership of Ellappa Govender. Over one hundred and fifty sculptures were produced, some expertly carved in semi-relief into niches of the tower, while others were made on the ground and then placed wherever a little ledge or corner could be found.

Darnell Shri Shiva Subrahmanya Alayam

Ramsamy Mudly, the owner of the Shiva Subrahmanya temple nearby, refused to open his temple to the public, whereupon the employees of the Huletts Sugar Mill decided to erect their own temple in 1912. The building was erected with funds deducted from each worker's pay packet. Ellappa Govender, who had some knowledge of temple building was responsible for the dome and sculpture.

In 1925 major alterations were carried out. A flat concrete roof or a tear behind parapets was removed and a gabled iron roof was installed in its place. This necessitated the removal of the parapet walls which only remnants at the four corners still exist in the 1970s a front veranda and various other structures were added. The building was originally painted in restrained cream but has been redecorated in garishly bright colors. The dome and plaster cornice work is beautifully executed although the general proportions are unfortunate. Kavady is the main festival.

All the weekend -builders had come from India and with vague memories of what sat on the temples at home, plus what one saw in Tongaat's toy shops, they set about constructing their own little wonderland. It was to be a Shiva Temple but with so many ledges, there was plenty of room left over for Vishnu, and Hanuman and Garuda and all the other; - and is that not Mr. Govender himself there right on the top, looking out over the landscape? Those lovely elephants in circus finery, one head and two bodies and those odd bulls - a very difficult junction, It says in the Silpa Sastras that idols should be dressed in the clothes of their region, not normally complied with by our local temple builders, but there are some really western - looking gentlemen on this tower. And then each one is painted, lovingly, beautifully, even Shiva and Parvati are given their own little house over the entrance. Two major alterations to the building, first the addition of an elegant veranda and later the construction of a "Spanish "screen wall, have detracted somewhat from the pure structure of the original building.

The interior still shows the magnificent understanding of architectural space which the builders must have possessed. There is first the main meeting room. Presumably, this was the only public space of the small community and was the gathering space where all matters of general interest were discussed. Here men, women, and children could meet, festivals were celebrated, and children were instructed in their mother tongue. Entrance is gained through a thick wall into the antaraca reserved for men and priests, while finally, a small opening leads to the cellar containing images of Subrahmanya, Shiva-Sakti, and the lingam.

There is a story that in 1929 there was an outbreak of malaria in Natal and that the local community was badly affected. A brahman was brought from Durban to perform a special ceremony. When this man saw the Subrahmanya idol inside the temple he informed the community that it was incorrectly sculpted and had to be removed. This was done at once and it was ceremoniously immersed in a nearby pond. within two months nearly one hundred people in the vicinity who had been suffering from malaria died, causing major upheavals in the community and no doubt, much fishing for the lost statue.

Before leaving the building and to gain some insight into the spatial concerns of these builders, it is worthwhile just to study the opening sequence leading to the main cella. A double door, set deeply into a heavily modulated external wall divides external from internal space. This is a large and generous opening well above human height and framed by protruding plaster piers and lintels. Around the frame, three simple, triangular recesses provide a place for sacrificial flames. The next opening is considerably smaller and lower. The number of recesses increases and the final opening is still narrower and lower, one has to stoop, and here even the floor rises. Ten triangular recesses now surround the opening. What a fantastic way to make spaces ever more private and precious.

Groutville Shiva Emperumal Temple

In complete contrast to the grandeur of the Tinley Manor temple is the private shrine of Perumal Naiker. It is situated in Groutville, a few kilometers further along the old main road to Stanger. It is put together from all the standard building elements of a North Coast - Edwardian hardware shop. Yet it is so lovingly done, so elegantly conceived and exquisitely sited that it achieves the same kind of 'presence' and image. Within the space of a few square meters, it incorporates all the main elements of the temple; the sikhara, mandapa, veranda, and Kodi pole, but still manages to retain a timeless simplicity.

New Guelderland Emperumal Temple

The original wood and iron temple was constructed in 1920 through the efforts of K Munian. The two present temples were built for the workers by Sugar Estate in 1958. The Shri Emperumal is flanked by the Mariamman Temple. The latter has locally made images of Durga, Banya Aman, and Mariamman. Major festivals Puratassi and Mariaman.

Mount Edgecombe Mariamman Temple

Reputedly built by the community over an existing anthill in 1890. Reconstructed in brick with funds donated by the company manager who had offered prayers at the temple on his way to work and had seen these answered by the birth of a child. The anthill is today over two meters high and is adorned with valuable jewellery during the annual Mariamman festival.

Illovo Mariamman Temple

The building is constructed of concrete blocks with an iron roof. It houses an interesting collection of religious prints and was built by the community in 1937. Rather lovely, naive sculpture adorns the gable end of the veranda. Kavady is celebrated at the end of January each year.

We are bound to our ancestors and to those who made us, whether we want to be or not. What matters is what we make of what we are. Our ancestors have invented, we can at least innovate. We rarely know who our ancestors were. Who can even remember the names of their great-grandparents? They have vanished into the dim and distant past.

Tinley Manor Siva Temple

The ancestors are very much invested in the children because the children are the ones who are going to continue the world that the ancestors made.

CHAPTER 2

This recycling of life continues until the soul finds its true nature. This is referred to as Brahma, which is their one God. Brahma has many forms. There are thousands of gods and goddesses that contain a part of Brahma. Many Hindus choose one or more of those gods to serve and worship.

This process can take many lifetimes. Therefore with each death, they strive to move closer to Brahma. They believe that when the body dies, the soul departs through the top of its head. It then lives on in a different form after a regrouping.

That form can be a human, animal, insect, or even plant. Hindus are avid believers of karma. They feel that by suffering, they cancel out past negative deeds. This is accomplished by fasting, confession, and intense prayer, to name a few.

Hindus are frequently seen with their heads shaved, which is a way for them to make sacrifices. Their karma helps to determine the form in which they are reborn in the next life

A number of days—between 10 and 16, after a person has "Reached the Abode of Siva," a special ceremony called a Kari yam is performed. Tamil tradition requires people to avoid saying that a person is dead. Instead, the person is said to have reached the world of Lord Siva, or to have reached the world of the dead or the ancestors.

It is believed that the recently departed soul, the subtle body, known as the ativahika-sarira, goes to Preta Loka (the world of ghosts and spirits). The Kariyam marks the transition for the soul from Preta Loka to Pitru Loka, the Abode of the Ancestors. Pitru Loka is that place where our ancestors reside until they get a physical body (reincarnate). It said that three of our previous generations reside in Pitru Loka, waiting to be born again. The Kariyam also marks the end of the time of mourning, and the most extreme restrictions for the family: refraining from cutting their fingernails, combing their hair, wearing jewelry or shoes, reading sacred texts, going to temples or to various celebratory functions, having sex, and cooking their own food. If all these restrictions are not properly honored, the soul may become a ghost that haunts its relatives

"Just as a man discards worn-out clothes and puts on new clothes, the soul discards worn-out bodies and wears new ones."

The twin beliefs of karma and reincarnation are among Hinduism's many jewels of knowledge. Others include dharma or our pattern of religious conduct, worshipful communion with God and Gods, the necessary guidance of the Sat Guru, and finally enlightenment through personal realization of our identity in and with God. So the strong-shouldered and keen-minded rishis knew and stated in the Vedas.

And these are not mere assumptions of probing, brilliant minds. They are laws of the cosmos. As God's force of gravity shapes cosmic order, karma shapes experiential order. Our long sequence of lives is a tapestry of creating and resolving karmas-positive, negative, and an amalgam of the two. During the succession of a soul's lives through the mysteries of our higher chakras and God's and Guru's Grace-no karmic situation will arise that exceeds an individual's ability to resolve it in love and understanding.

Many people are very curious about their past lives and expend great time, effort, and money to explore them. This curious probing into past lives is unnecessary. Indeed it is a natural protection from reliving past trauma or becoming infatuated more with our past lives than our present life that the inner recesses of the Muladhara memory chakra are not easily accessed. For, as we exist now is a sum total of all our past lives. In our present moment, our mind and body state is the cumulative result of the entire spectrum of our past lives. So, no matter how great the intellectual knowledge of these two key principles, it is how we currently live that positively shapes karma and unfolds us spiritually. Knowing the laws, we are responsible to resolve blossoming karmas from past lives and create karma that, projected into the future, will advance, not hinder us.

Karma literally means "deed or act," but more broadly describes the principle of cause and effect. Simply stated, karma is the law of action and reaction that governs consciousness. In physics-the study of energy and matter-Sir, Isaac Newton postulated that for every action there is an equal and opposite reaction. Push against a wall. Its material is molecularly pushing back with a force exactly equal to yours. In metaphysics, karma is the law that states that every mental, emotional, and physical activity, no matter how insignificant, is projected out into the psychic mind substance and eventually returns to the individual with equal impact.

The akashic memory in our higher chakras faithfully records the soul's impressions during its series of earthly lives, and in the astral/mental worlds in-between earth existences. Ancient yogis, in psychically studying the timeline of cause/effect, assigned three categories to karma. The first is sanchita, the sum total of past karma yet to be resolved. The second category is prarabdha, that portion of sanchita karma being experienced in the present life. Kriyamana, the third type, is karma you are presently creating. However, it must be understood that your past negative karma can be altered into a smoother, easier state through the loving, heart-chakra nature, through dharma and sadhana. That is the key to karmic wisdom. Live religiously well and you will create positive karma for the future and soften negative karma of the past. Truths and Myths About Karma

Karma operates not only individually, but also in ever-enlarging circles of group karma where we participate in the sum karma of multiple souls. This includes family, community, nation, race and religion, even planetary group karma. So if we, individually or collectively, unconditionally love and give, we will be loved and given to. The individuals or groups who act soulfully or maliciously toward us are the vehicles of our own karmic creation. The people who manifest your karma are also living through past karma and simultaneously creating future karma. For example, if their karmic pattern did not include miserliness, they would not be involved in your karma of selfishness. Another person may express some generosity toward you, fulfilling the gifting karma of your past experience. Imagine how intricately interconnected all the cycles of karma are for our planet's life forms.

Many people believe in the principle of karma, but don't apply its laws to their daily life or even to life's peak experiences. There is a tendency to cry during times of personal crisis, "Why has God done this to me?" or "What did I do to deserve this?" While God is the creator and sustainer of the cosmic law of karma, He does not dispense individual karma. He does not produce cancer in one person's body and develops Olympic athletic prowess in another's. We create our own experiences. It is really an exercise of our soul's powers of creation. Karma, then, is our best spiritual teacher. We spiritually learn and grow as our actions return to us to be resolved and dissolved. In this highest sense, there is no good and bad karma; there is the self-created experience that presents opportunities for spiritual advancement. If we can't draw lessons from karma, then we resist and/or resent it, lashing out with mental, emotional, or physical force. The original substance of that karmic event is spent and no longer exists, but the current reaction creates a new condition of harsh karma.

Responsibility resolving karma is among the most important reasons that a Sat Guru is necessary for a sincere seeker's life. The Guru helps the devotee to hold his mind in focus, to become pointedly conscious of thought, word and deed. Without the guidance and grace of the Guru, the devotee's mind will be splintered between instinctive and intellectual forces, making it very difficult to resolve karma. Only when karma is wisely harnessed can the mind become still enough to experience its own superconscious depths.

Karma is also misunderstood as fate, an unchangeable destiny decreed long ago by agencies or forces external to us such as the planet and stars, or Gods. Karma is neither fate nor predetermination. Each soul has absolute free will Its only boundary is karma. God and Gods do not dictate the experiential events of our lives, nor do they test us. And there is no cosmic force that moulds our life. Indeed, when beseeched through deep prayer and worship, the Supreme Being and His great Gods may intercede within our karma, lightening its impact or shifting its location in time to a period when we are better prepared to resolve it. Hindu astrology, or Jyotisha, details a real relation between ourselves and the geography of the solar system and certain star clusters, but it is not a cause-effect relation. Planets and stars don't cause or dictate karma. Their orbital relationships establish proper conditions for karmas to activate and a particular type of personality nature to develop. Jyotisha describes a relation of revealment: it reveals prarabdha karmic patterns for a given birth and how we will generally react to them (kriyamana karma). This is like a pattern of different colored windows allowing sunlight to reveal and color a house's arrangement of furniture. With astrological knowledge, we are aware of our life's karmic pattern and can thereby anticipate it wisely. Reincarnation: A Soul's Path to Goodness

The soul dwells as the inmost body of light and superconscious, the universal mind of a series of nested bodies, each more refined than the next: physical, pranic, astral, mental. In our conscious mind, we think and feel ourselves to be a physical body with some intangible spirit within it. Yet, right now our real identity is the soul that is sensing through its multiple bodies physical, emotional, and mental experience. Recognizing this as reality, we powerfully know that life doesn't end with the death of the biological body. The soul continues to occupy the astral body, a subtle, luminous duplicate of the physical body. This subtle body is made of higher-energy astral matter and dwells in a dimension called the astral plane. If the soul body itself is highly evolved, it will occupy the astral/mental bodies on a very refined plane of the astral known as the Devaloka, "the world of light-shining beings." At death, the soul slowly becomes totally aware of its astral/mental bodies and it predominantly lives through those bodies in the astral dimension.

The soul functions with complete continuity in its astral/mental bodies. It is with these sensitive vehicles that we experience dream or "astral" worlds during sleep every night. The astral world is equally as solid and beautiful, as varied and comprehensive as the earth dimension-if not much more so. Spiritual growth, psychic development, guidance in matters of governance and commerce, artistic cultivation, inventions and discoveries of medicine, science, and technology all continue by astral people who are "in-between" earthly lives. Many of the Veda hymns entreat the assistance of devas: advanced astral or mental people. Yet, also in the grey, lower regions of this vast, invisible dimension exist astral people whose present pursuits are base, selfish, even sadistic. Where the person goes in the astral plane at sleep or death is dependent upon his earthly pursuits and the quality of his mind.

Because certain seed karmas can only be resolved in earth consciousness and because the soul's initial realizations of Absolute Reality are only achieved in a physical body, our soul joyously enters another biological body. At the right time, it is reborn into a flesh body that will best fulfill its karmic pattern. In this process, the current astral body-which is a duplicate of the last physical form-is sluffed off as a lifeless shell that in due course disintegrates, and a new astral body develops as the new physical body grows. This entering into another body is called reincarnation: "re-occupying the flesh."

During our thousands of earth lives, a remarkable variety of life patterns are experienced. We exist as male and female, often switching back and forth from life to life as nature becomes more harmonized into a person exhibiting both feminine nurturing and masculine intrepidness. We come to earth as princesses and presidents, as paupers and pirates, as tribals and scientists, as for murderers and healers, as atheists and, ultimately, God-realized sages. We take bodies of every race and live the many religions, faiths, and philosophies as the soul gains more knowledge and evolutionary experience.

Therefore, the Hindu knows that the belief in a single life on earth, followed by eternal joy or pain is utterly wrong and causes great anxiety, confusion, and fear. Hindus know that all souls reincarnate, take one body and then another, evolving through experience over long periods of time. Like the caterpillar's metamorphosis into the butterfly, death doesn't end our existence but frees us to pursue an even greater development.

Understanding the laws of the death process, the Hindu is vigilant of his thoughts and mental loyalties. He knows that the contents of his mind at the point of death in large part dictate where he will function in the astral plane and the quality of his next birth. Secret questionings and doubt of Hindu belief, and associations with other belief systems will automatically place him among like-minded people whose beliefs are alien to Hinduism. A nominal Hindu on earth could be a selfish materialist in the astral world. The Hindu also knows that death must come naturally, in its own course, and that suicide only accelerates the intensity of one's karma, bringing a series of immediate lesser births and requiring several lives for the soul to return to the exact evolutionary point that existed at the moment of suicide, at which time the still-existing karmic entanglements must again be faced and resolved.

Two other karmically sensitive processes are: 1.) artificially sustaining life in a wholly incapacitated physical body through mechanical devices, drugs, or intravenous feeding; and 2.) euthanasia, "mercy killing." There is a critical timing in the death transition. The dying process can involve long-suffering or be peaceful or painfully sudden: all dependent on the karma involved. To keep a person on life support with the sole intent of continuing the body's biological functions nullifies the natural timing of death. It also keeps the person's astral body earthbound, tethered to a lower astral region rather than being released into higher astral levels.

An important lesson to learn here is that karma is conditioned by intent. When the medical staff receives a dangerously ill or injured person and they place him on life support as part of an immediate life-saving procedure, their intent is pure healing. If their attempts are unsuccessful, then the life-support devices are turned off, the person dies naturally and there is no karma involved and it does not constitute euthanasia. However, if the doctors, family, or patient decide to continue life support indefinitely to prolong biological processes, (usually motivated by a Western belief of single life) then the intent carries full karmic consequences. When a person is put on long-term life support, he must be left on it until some natural biological or environmental event brings death. If he is killed through euthanasia, this again further disturbs the timing of the death. As a result, the timing of future births would be drastically altered.

Euthanasia, the willful destruction of a physical body, is very serious karma. This applies to all cases including someone experiencing long-term, intolerable pain. Even such difficult life experiences must be allowed to resolve themselves naturally. Dying may be painful, but death itself is not. All those involved (directly or indirectly) in euthanasia will proportionately take on the remaining prarabdha karma of the dying person. And the euthanasia participants will, to the degree contributed, face a similar karmic situation in this or a future life.

Finally, there is exercising wisdom-which is knowing and using divine law in the overall context of any situation For example, a vegetative person in a coma is on long-term life support in a hospital when a patient is brought in for emergency treatment requiring that same life support equipment. Weighing the two karmas, a doctor could harmonically unplug the comatose patient in order to save the other's life. Moksha: Freedom From Rebirth

Life's real attainment is not money, not a material luxury, not sexual or eating pleasure, not intellectual, business or political power, or any other of the instinctive or intellectual needs. These are natural pursuits, to be sure, but our divine purpose on this earth is to personally realize our identity in and with God. This is now called by many names: enlightenment, Self-Realization, God-Realization, and Nirvikalpa Samadhi. After many lifetimes of wisely controlling the creation of karma and resolving past karmas when they return, the soul is fully matured in the knowledge of these divine laws and the highest use of them. Through the practice of yoga, the Hindu bursts into God's superconscious Mind, the experience of bliss, all-knowingness, perfect silence. His intellect is transmuted, and he soars into the Absolute Reality of God. He is a jnani, a knower of the Known. When the jnani is stable in repeating his realization of the

Absolute, there is no longer a need for physical birth, for all lessons have been learned, all karmas fulfilled and Godness is his natural mental state. That individual soul is then naturally liberated, freed from the cycle of birth, death & rebirth on this planet. After Moksha, our soul continues its evolution in the inner worlds, eventually merging back into its origin: God, the Primal Soul.

Every Hindu expects to seek for and attain moksha. But he or she does not expect that it will necessarily come in this present life. Hindus know this and do not delude themselves that this life is the last. Seeking and attaining profound spiritual realizations, they nevertheless know that there is much to be accomplished on earth and that only mature, God-realized souls attain Moksha.

God may seem distant and remote as the experience of our self-created karmas clouds our mind. Yet, in reality, the Supreme Being is always closer to you than the beat of your heart. His Mind pervades the totality of your karmic experience and lifetimes. As karma is God's cosmic law of cause and effect, dharma is God's law of Being, including the pattern of Hindu religiousness. Through the following dharma and controlling thought, word and deed, karma is harnessed and wisely created. You become the master, the knowing creator, not a helpless victim. Through being consistent in our religiousness, following the yamas and niyamas (Hindu restraints and observances), performing the Pancha Nitya karmas (five constant duties), seeing God everywhere and in everyone, our past karma will soften. We may experience karma indirectly through seeing someone else going through a situation that we intuitively know was karma we also were to face. But because of devout religiousness, we may experience it vicariously or in lesser intensity. For example, physical karma may manifest as a mental experience or a realistic dream; an emotional karmic storm may just barely touch our minds before dying out.

The belief in karma and reincarnation brings to each Hindu inner peace and self-assurance. The Hindu knows that the maturing of the soul takes many lives and that if the soul is immature in the present birth, then there is hope, for there will be many opportunities for learning and growing in future lives. Yes, these beliefs and the attitudes they produce eliminate anxiety, giving the serene perception that everything is all right as it is. And, there is also a keen insight into the human condition and appreciation for people in all stages of spiritual unfoldment.

CHAPTER 3

The 60s Apartheid Era in South Africa

Grace was born on 5th August 1965 at St Aidans Hospital in Durban, Natal, South Africa.

History of St Aidans as was in those days.

Rev Dr. Lancelot Parker Booth (1850-1925)

St Aidan's Mission Regional Hospital rose from the missionary work of the Rev. Dr. Lancelot Parker Booth. He had arrived in Natal, from England, at a period when thousands of indentured Indians laborers were imported to work on sugar plantations. When their term of indenture expired, many settled in Durban. He was appalled at the conditions of the Indian laboring classes, particularly at the poverty, illiteracy, the low standard of living, the lack of medical facilities, and he felt the urgent need for their spiritual upliftment.

In 1886 Booth's "Mission Schools" were established in Durban where subsequently thousands of the poorer Indian children, whether Christian or non-Christian, could receive the rudiments of education. In the following year, the St Aidan's Church was completed.

Booth, as Diocesan Superintendent of Indian Missions in Natal, desired to reach out to the greater Indian population. He perceived that the greatest need lay in medical services for the underprivileged classes. Consequently, in the backyard of the Mission House, he opened a dispensary where he could attend to the medical needs of thousands of the poorer citizens of Durban.

Dr. Booth and after 1883-1900-1915

When Rev. Dr. Booth left Durban in June 1900, 837 local Indians presented him with a "Special Tribute". Although the signatories of this unique document refer to Booth's "Hospital', ironically Booth did not establish a hospital. Instead, at his dispensary at 49 Cross Street, he treated thousands of out-patients because to date, neither the State nor the Municipality had made any effort to provide hospital facilities for the Indian population.

By modern standards, medical science was still in its infancy by 1900. In the sub-tropical climate of Natal, the disease was prevalent but the position was aggravated by slum conditions, overcrowding, unhygienic living, poverty, ignorance, and "superstition". Medical missionaries throughout the world were convinced that Western medicine was the strongest means at their disposal to bring Christianity nearer to the masses.

Dr. Booth was also a pioneer in introducing nursing and first-aid to Indian men. The Indian Stretcher-Bearer Corps, which he trained for service in the Anglo-Boer War, was a unique contribution to South African medical history. Perhaps, he was stimulated by M.K. Gandhi in this venture. Furthermore, Booth's influence caused Sergeant-Major Gandhi to form another volunteer group for service in the 1906 Zulu Uprising. There is also speculation that St Aidan's provided. A Red Cross group during World War 1, but this is subject to further research.

With the departure of Dr. Booth, many local doctors such as Drs. Robinson, his wife Lillian Robinson, Stanley Copley, Francois, and Mundy attended to the medical needs of the poor in the period 1900-1907. Meanwhile, the S.P.G. also made its contribution. Between 1904 and 1906 Nurse Richnell arrived to be followed by Dr. Ethel Pryce (1907-9). There must have been a need for medical services because the number of dispensaries increased. Although the Cross Street dispensary was closed in 1906, new ones were established at Sydenham and Springfield and in 1916, at Overport.

3RD HOSPITAL 1935-1983

On 16 January 1935, the foundation stone of the present hospital was laid by Kunwarani Lady Maharaj Singh, wife of the then Agent-General for the Government of India. On July 4 the hospital was formally opened by the Countess of Clarendon, the wife of Governor-General of the Union of South Africa. The building was designed by Mr. W.B. Oxley and erected by Messrs Tedder and Brown. The initial stages of the building program had cost approximately R20 000 and by 1940 the hospital had accommodation for 60 patients.

From this date onwards, the history of the hospital is a continuous record of expansion, increasing staff, introducing up-to-date medical equipment, and very importantly, acquiring additional funds. Fortunately, the Indian public too had become aware of the important role which St Aidan's Hospital was destined to play in the life of the Indian community. Among the early benefactors were the R.K. Khan Trust, M.E. and M.A. Motola, and the Rustomjee Trust which, in 1938, contributed towards the installation of modern X-Ray equipment. Men and women of all races and religions came together in a great effort to alleviate sickness and suffering. In an age, before medical societies came to be accepted as the norm, the Hospital provided a great service for rich and poor alike. In 1940 the Rev. Satchell was one of the founders of the Friends of the Sick Association (F.O.S.A) which still exists today.

The Diocese aware of its responsibilities and aware of the great social and material upliftment which had taken place in the Indian community over the past eighty years, passed a Resolution (ACT 11 of 1946) which henceforth placed the administration of the hospital under a BOARD of MANAGEMENT. This board consisted of 12 members, six of whom were elected by the Synod and the remaining six would be elected by the INDIAN MEDICAL SERVICES TRUST. The Bishop would act ex officio as Chairman or alternatively, a Deputy Chairman appointed by the Bishop would preside (at present the Rector of St Aidan's Parish). The Indian Medical Services Trust, established on 22 July 1947 and registered on 29 September 1947, represented the interests of the Indian community and was composed of doctors, merchants, and persons from the professions. Dr. K.M. Seedat was the first Chairman of the Trust and in this capacity, he collected R48 000 from the Indian community for the second phase of the development of the new hospital.

Aware of the acute shortage of accommodation, the Board of Management embarked on an R76 000 program of expansion. During 1948/49 plans were completed and in August 1949 extensions commenced. On 22 September 1951, the new extensions were officially opened by the Hon. Mr. M.G. Shepstone, Administrator of Natal. By 1952 the hospital had accommodation for 100 beds. When completed the central building appeared as a rectangle with a large central square as a garden. The extensions had cost R75 287.50 and the Natal Provincial Administration contributed two-thirds of the total cost.

In May 1952 Miss L. Pratt and Mis E. Hart laid the foundation stone of the St. Luke's Chapel which adjoined the hospital. It is this Christian aspect that has given St. Aidan's mission its special characteristic. The hospital admits all races as patients and employs multi-racial staff. It offers facilities for the training of nurses. At present 157 local doctors and specialists visit their patients at the hospital. There are three types of patients, full fee-paying, part fee-paying, and ten percent of the beds are reserved for indigent patients. During each decade the hospital has striven to offer the most up-to-date facilities and patients can be accommodated in private as well as general wards. In 1960 the Hospital faced an entirely new problem- the Group Areas Act, which declared the Hospital a "Special Zone" and for many years the Board sought permission to undertake further "extensions". In 1966 the new St Aidan's church was built on a plot adjoining the hospital. By 1970 when the Natal Indian population had reached 500 000, patients' accommodation had reached acute proportions but residence for nurses was perhaps the most urgent priority. The hospital is one of the oldest in Durban.

Her mum said it was a difficult birth as she was a premature baby, and had to stay in an incubator for a few weeks. Grace was very tiny and her dad said he could carry her in a shoebox. Her mum stayed a few days in the hospital, where it was run by nuns. They were very kind to her mum and prayed over Grace while she was in the incubator fighting for her life. Her mum said she had almost lost her, but Grace was a fighter and that the nuns named her Grace (The **name Grace** means Charm and is of Latin origin. The name **Grace** was first bestowed as a reference to the "**grace** of God.")

When her mum arrived home with Grace, they had to do prayers and they chose the name Thirupurasundari (Thiru), named after the doctor who helped bring her into the world.

She was the fourth child and there were children altogether. Grace had two brothers and two sisters. Her mum said that they used to take Grace by the legs and massage people who were sick, as she was born bridged and the saying goes 'those born bridged are lucky people and have a gift of healing.'

The first memory of Grace and her surroundings was when she was 3 years old.

They lived in a place called Gum Tree Road, Sea Cow Lake. The name Sea Cow Lake is the only memory of the animals that roamed the banks of the Umgeni River.

"Not far above the Umgeni bridge, on the northern side of the river, is Sea Cow Lake, which in the early days of the (Port Natal) settlement was a lake of no small pretensions, in which sea cows (hippopotamus) were of common occurrence, but now it is merely a reedy swamp."

Grace's grandparents lived not far away in Valley Road, high up on the hills of the Umgeni River. The long and dusty graveled, the windy road led to her grandparent's house. The house stood on top of the hill overlooking the **Umgeni River.**

Grace could see people swimming in the river, while little boats rowed past them. It looked magnificent, this huge river flowing eloquently, The beauty of nature, surrounded by age-old trees swaying gently with the wind.

The house itself was made of corrugated iron and tin, surrounded by luscious fruit and vegetable trees. There were mangoes, banana, guava, and pawpaw trees. There were tomatoes and mealie trees. The land was bursting with life from the earth, all grown by her grandparents.

The house had four well-furnished bedrooms and a separate building for the kitchen which had a coal stove and a table with chairs. The toilet and bathroom were outside in another section of the yard. The taps were outside as well, her grandma washed dishes and carried them back to the kitchen. Her thatha brought the coal to the kitchen for the stove and aiya boiled water for everyone to bathe. The clothes were washed outside, dried on the washing line outside on the side of the house. The buckets were made of steel to use water to bathe. There was no electricity, oil and paraffin lamps were used.

The children played hide and seek, while the ducks and fowls watched over their little ones. The dogs lazed under the trees next to their kennels.

Grace's thatha was a very quiet, well-dressed gentleman. He used to get up very early and got the coal for her aiya then lit the stove for her to start the day's cooking. Aiya would make his tea and make his lunch for work. He worked at The National Chemical Product Factory. The factory was down the hill into the valley where her thatha walked to work and back every day. Thatha was a Vaishnavite, who worshipped in his built temple in Valley Road.

Surprisingly, Grace never saw him drinking, spirits. he did smoke the pipe. He spoke very little, a man of few words. He played the violin and read the newspapers in the evenings after he had eaten his dinner. Traditionally men were served their dinner first, then the children, and last were the women. Thatha appeared to be a well-educated man.

All the children respected him and were in awe when in his presence. Grace loved listening to him play the violin. It was comforting to listen to him play for them. Sometimes it was sad and other times it was lively and happy. Grace often wondered who her thatha was thinking of when he used to play the violin. He seemed to disappear into his own world and his fingers meticulously fiddled away.

Other days Grace would find her thatha in the garden digging and planting seeds for the new crops. Mealies on the cob were her favorite, freshly taken from its tree, it was sweet and succulent.

Growing up there were many folktales about the brave men and women of those times that have passed away.

The heroes of the Umgeni

This is a story of courage and of tragedy- the courage of six men, with dogged determination, who defied the wrath of nature when destruction struck the Umgeni Valley in 1917.

Torrential rains continued for four consecutive days. On Sunday 28th October, the sleepers of the Umgeni Valley were awakened by a most thunderous din as the raging rose rapidly and beleaguered the numerous houses. Many perished in their sleep, while others scrambled to rooftops. Here, whipped by the downpour howling wind that had reached hurricane force, they clung desperately as the foundations of their homes were rocked by the swirling torrents.

In such a hazardous and precarious plight, many clung on as they swelted the morning light and hope of rescues. Throughout the night, the river rose rapidly and the clogging of the debris at the bridges dammed the furious on-rushing waters and set up a number of treacherous cross-currents throughout the inundated area.

The whole Umgeni Valley presented a picture of utter desolation. The surging water was pounding furiously against the Connaught Bridge. As the river currents proved too dangerous, the Chief Constable decided to abandon further rescue work. It was at this critical moment that the famous Padavatan brothers, Mariemuthoo and Gengan, together with their companions, Valoo, Sabapathy Govender, Rungasamy Naidoo, and Kupusamy Naidoo decided to render help.

Although these people were accustomed to riding the swells of the seas, the river currents proved too treacherous. Nevertheless, the split-second teamwork, able leadership, and the determination to save lives were rewarding. During each trip, they brought loads of 30 to 40 persons. After five trips, they were restrained from further attempts as the light was failing and they were exhausted. Altogether they rescued 175 people.

The great deluge left in its wake a deplorable scene of death, destruction, and devastation The local press paid tribute to this courageous and memorable rescue in recognition of this gallant feat, the citizens of Durban gave each of these heroes a gold medal bearing Durban's Coat of Arms. In addition, a silver-mounted Malacca Stick was presented to the Captain of the team. The sentiments of the Indian community were aptly recorded in a citation presented to Mariemuthoo in appreciation and gratitude for their heroic services.

****

Her Aiya was the opposite, she was always laughing and would often let Grace comb her hair whilst she sang devotional songs. Aiya had long beautiful straight hair and wore colorful sarees. She had these beautiful gold earrings and bangles that made a tinkling sound every time she moved her dainty hands. Her love for God and pride in the temple that thatha had built for her stood magnificently in the yard. Aiya was a holy woman, hundreds of people came from near and far to get their fortunes read and blessings from aiya. Grace would often help in the temple, washing the deities and dressing them up with colorful materials made of silk. Aiya was a Shaivite and worshiped at home and at the Umgeni Road which is a Siva Temple

Grace's love for God was instilled in her ever since she remembers as a young child. Aiya and her mum, with Grace following them, would go to the temple in the yard and spend a long time cleaning the brass chomboos, trays for turning camphor, and the 'Gods' made of brass. Her mum and her aiya would scrub it and polish it till she could see her reflection. Her mum and Aiya would sing devotional songs as they worked in the temple. Grace loved listening to them sing and soon she was humming along with them.

The days were spent singing and playing musical instruments with them. Grace loved it all. The temple was so colorful with the 'God's all washed and dressed in sarees just like mum and aiya. Evening came and the family would gather in the temple and sing and play musical instruments. One of the cousins recalls this memory of aiya telling them of her parents.

" His name was Sriram Reddy- a sheep and goat herder. They resided in Fairbreeze, Tongaat, and were very rich. They lived not far from the river. Anybody who wanted to buy livestock came to him for advice and assistance. Even the White farmers came to him and gave him money and trusted him in choosing and purchasing goats. Grandma used to sell stuff also. Sometime between 1915 and 1920, there was a massive flood. They had to leave all their things and flee. Amongst those things were tins full of sovereigns. Grandma said, " what about the money?" He replied " money, we can make it, let's go " putting Aiya on his shoulders, he crossed the river. Aiya was about eleven years old at the time" (Aiya's Father)

Grace loved her Aiya with every breath she was 'God' in every way, shape, and form. Aiya made Grace laugh so much and her attempt to speak English.

Grace's family lived a few streets away from her grandparents' house. They had to walk through bushes to visit her grandparents which was a highlight in young Grace's life.

Her dad was a musician in the band called Kalaivani Orchestra for over twenty years and the band members split up when Grace was quite young.

Grace had heard many stories and anecdotes about the "family band", its music, the occasions and venues at which it performed, and the incidents that shaped its development. Intrigued by this wealth of oral information Grace decided to continue with her research on her grand heritage her ancestors left behind

At least ninety percent of the musicians in those times never reached high school. Those that did, did so with a great deal of family and personal sacrifice. Education was not compulsory and going to school, it seems, was a luxury that meant having the requisite funds for school fees, textbooks, writing material, and school uniforms. All orchestral musicians came from large working-class families and at some point had to leave school in order to support their families. As a result, most Indian musicians (and many non-musicians for that matter) entered the labor ~ market at very early ages. One of the most important ways in which a musician was identified was by the family from which he came. If his uncles, brothers, or father were well-known musicians, into this meant an automatic entry for him the orchestral tradition

Indian music, like the music of many other cultures, is an integral part of the. the lifestyle of the people it represents. In South Africa however, this aspect of music was used by the apartheid government in its quest to. emphasize separate development. Indian music, especially in the seventies and eighties when the political situation seemed most volatile, was viewed in favorable terms by the government, since it was seen as "belonging" to Indian people and as such, maintaining, if not reinforcing their Indianness.

In other words, it was used as an effective political tool by the apartheid regime to further "Indianize" and thus de-Westernize the image of Indian people. As a result, there was massive state support in the eight~es for the introduction of Indian music into Indian schools

The political situation as being volatile in the seventies and eighties, The incidents such as the student riots that took place in Soweto in 1976, the declaration of a State of Emergency by the South African government in 1986, and the acts of violence that erupted subsequent to both these incidents

The Kalaivani Orchestra originated from Mount EdgecombeThe group was made up of sugar mill workers living in the barracks My dad grew up in Mount Edgecombe and his family was workers of the sugar mill. They lived in the barracks on the plantation, and his parents worked at the sugar plantation. In Mount Edgecombe, indentured migrants occupied tent-like homes near the temple, and workers were housed in the sugar mill. Some of the structures had existed for more than a hundred years before the newer structure near Campbelltown and the surrounding areas came about.

The community at Mount Edgecombe was a poor one where entertainment was an important part of daily life. However, with the introduction of upmarket estates, the fortunes of people living there today are very different from what they were many years ago.

Grace's dad was a very lovely person and often made people smile with his singing. He had a great talent both as a musician and an artist (painting and sketching). Her dad could paint anything, he was so gifted and painted on her mum's plain saree and turned it into a masterpiece. Her dad would take his guitar, his eyes would shine and the atmosphere in the house was so electric with happiness and joy. And all would gather around him, children turned up from around the neighborhood and all danced happily while her dad gave them a live show. The band split up when she was born, and her dad was out of work for a long time. He spent his days painting and singing, whilst playing the guitar.

Her mum was a beautiful woman who worked very hard as a machinist in a clothing factory. And she sewed clothes for the girls and herself. She had jet black, straight long hair always neatly tied in a plait. She was slender in build and is fair in complexion.

She would come home very tired, do the cooking and keep the home clean. She tried her best with the little income she fed the family of seven, as Grace's dad was no longer in the band and things got harder to support the family. Her dad did not have any other skill except being a musician and an artist so work was scarce and the family was very poor.

Her mum found another job and she taught in the nursery school down the road from Gum Tree Road, where they lived. Her mum taught her how to read and write and how to spell words. They used to walk hand in hand down the hill and crossed the main road to the school. Grace played with the other children and they would sing and do traditional dancing. They used to go to her aiya and thatha every other day, it was about a mile away and the family had to walk through bushes and long grass to reach their house.

"From every wound, there is a scar, and every scar tells a story. A story that says, -I survived."

CHAPTER 4

The 70's

Grace's mum and dad applied for a council house and waited a long time before they got the news. The family moved to the new house in another town called Chatsworth, Grace was seven years old then and started primary school, her mum went back as a machinist to work.

Chatsworth is a historically Indian township located in Durban some 14km southwest of the city center, in the Umhlatuzana River Valley, north of Umlazi. Initially, it consisted mainly of poor, working-class Indian people, whose culture is central to Durban's identity, and a direct result of the Group Areas Act. Chatsworth comprises an area that was once a farm called Chatsworth, part of Witteklip, which was acquired in 1848 by one Samuel Bennington and named by him after Chatsworth near Chesterfield in Derbyshire, England.

Who would ever imagine the little girl Grace would end up in England and visit all the places that linked her to the past.

Everyone was so excited because finally, the children would get their own rooms. It was far away from Grace's grandparent's house and Grace missed those visits. Her mum took the children to visit their grandparents by bus whenever her mum had some spare money.

Her dad still hadn't found a job. The house was lovely, it had a big yard with three bedrooms upstairs and a dining room, lounge, and kitchen downstairs. It even had a bathroom and two toilets indoors. It was like living in a castle for Grace All the houses around them looked alike in neat rows and they stood behind one another. Still, there was no electricity as there wasn't enough money to pay for it.

Grace started primary school and walked almost 2 miles every day to school and back. Soon the house was filled with people as her cousins moved in to help with finances. There were over ten people in the house at one time. Grace and her siblings had to share rooms again. Her dad painted lovely sceneries on the bare walls and floors. Her mum went back to work in the factory, and she had to travel by train to get to work. Grace used to walk with her to the train station when Grace was a bit older. In the evening s Grace would sit on the step at the back door and watch for the train to come and would run to meet her mum when she saw the train come to the station.

Her dad finally found a job in a paint manufacturing company and started to do things for the house. He used to bring home the gallons of paint and let the children help paint the house. Her dad used to buy paint for all the neighbors. When her dad was off he would often play the guitar and sing for the children. The neighborhood children used to gather at their house and they would have a disco with live music.

Grace's mum drew her courage and strength from her belief and faith in God. Her mum woke up early hours before sunrise and lifted her hands to the sun every single day without fail. Grace would go with her mum to the temple and learn to play musical instruments, and Tamil songs to praise God. Grace and her mum found peace in the temple. It was a sanctuary for both of them. Grace used to help clean the temple, clean the lamp, and make garlands. These were to be the only cherished memories of quality time spent with her mum. It brought them closer to God and their love for each other grew spiritually.

Grace put all her energy into school and temple life.

Those places were her sanctuary, a place to be at peace and free. She was fascinated with all the books that were available to her, it opened a whole new world where she could escape to. Grace admired the Madams in colorful saree and the Sirs in fine-cut suits and ties. Grace looked up to them for love and support. She began to shine in her class and excelled both academically and in sports. Grace started getting recognized for her achievements at school and was often awarded sweets, certificates, and trophies.

Grace made lots of friends at school and often went to her friend's homes after school. Grace was always hungry and her friend's mum fed her often. Grace grew to be a favorite to one of the Madam in school, so Grace told her about her life at home. The madam took her under her wings during school hours, brought her a packed lunch, and showed her love. She often gave Grace hugs which were rare at her home.

At home, her cousins moved out to their own place, her siblings and she had more space once again. The girls shared a bedroom, whilst the boys shared the other bedroom.

There were many happy days when Grace and her friends played outdoors- building playhouses out of tree branches, playing hopscotch, and skipping rope. Grace learned to play football and cricket and played marbles with her brothers when they were in a good mood.

Things were becoming harder at home, children were growing up and life was getting more and more expensive. The electricity was cut off a few times and Grace had to do homework using a candle.

Her mum was her hero, her faith in God never faltered and she instilled in Grace that people would let her down but God is omnipresent and always in the hearts. She believed her mum and that one day it would get better.

Her mum and she went to the temple down the road. It was in a big tent up on the hill of the road. There were many people that came to the temple. It was at the temple that Grace learned the instruments, thallium, tambourine, and harmonica. She knew the songs by heart.

Grace was confused about who God was, the kitchen door neighbor was a Christian and they had a God called Jesus. The side neighbor was a Muslim and they had a God called Allah. The front of the house was the same as Grace's family. They went to the same temple and prayed to Lord Shiva. To Grace, it didn't matter. She longed to please God so she went to the church, read the namaz, and sang to Lord Shiva. To her young mind, God was everywhere.

The year was 1977, in the Indian township of Chatsworth, Grace had just started high school. She was always excited about school as this is where she was always happy. Grace made friends easily and she always walked to school with her friend, Naomi. This morning Grace felt very sick in the pit of her stomach, she knew something horrible was about to happen but there was no way she could prevent this from happening. Grace often found her dreams and visions coming true, so this particular vision had shaken her up so bad that when she entered her friend's house that morning, she was weak and shaking. Naomi got scared and told Grace that they would stay home together.

I AM DEAD - THEY KILLED ME……

They sat in the lounge watching television when Naomi's uncle came in and said that he would take Grace home. Both the girls jumped up in fright, yet followed the uncle out of the house, they all got into his car and he drove away. He drove the girls around for miles before stopping at a deserted spot on the beach. There was not a single car or person on sight. He got out of the car and grabbed Grace and pulled her out first. Naomi seeing this, started screaming and ran off, leaving Grace with her uncle.

Grace started to scream and pull away from the uncle but was too little to fight back. The uncle slapped and punched Grace in her stomach and Grace was on the sand writhing in pain. The uncle then continued to beat Grace, tore at her school dress, and raped her numerous times. Grace was in and out of consciousness, she could hear his grunts and his heavy breathing on her. What seemed like hours the silence was what made Grace open her eyes. Grace let out a loud, piercing scream when she saw the blood on her white school dress. She got herself up, slowly with her feet dragging, she walked into the sea. She had to end it all. But life had a purpose so the sea washed her ashore.

As she tried to get up from the sand, Grace called out to her friend. The wind carried the sounds of crying and Grace rushed towards the crying. She eventually found Naomi, hiding in the bushes, crying and bleeding in her mouth and her clothes soaked in blood.

Her uncle had hurt them badly. Grace gathered her strength, grabbed Naomi and took her to the water, and helped her wash. Naomi was a year older than Grace, yet it was Grace that did all the thinking and planning to get out of there.

Naomi would not stop crying. Grace told her they would have to find a way home before their parents found out they were missing. The girls managed to drag themselves to the highway and a passerby stopped and took the girls to the bus stop.

The trip on the bus was a silent one between the two friends. They made a silent pact never to reveal what had happened, as they both did not go to school that morning, they would be in a lot of trouble. Naomi finally broke her silence by repeating not to tell anyone as it was her uncle that had harmed them. They parted their ways and were never able to remain friends after that.

Grace returned to her house, and no one even noticed the bruises on her face and legs. Grace's personality changed from that day onwards. Grace could no longer concentrate on her studies, she used to wet the bed and had terrible nightmares of drowning and being killed by the bogeyman. She joined the outcasts at schools and became a rebel. Her parents were often called to the school and Grace was given chances to stay as teachers knew that something had happened to Grace for her to change so drastically.

However, in those days, no one spoke about the abuse and it seemed normal for an Indian girl child to be treated as such.

Grace would go on to meet a young lad and take a liking to him. But he was Christian and She was a Tamil girl, so that relationship was out of bounds. Her parents found out that she was meeting this boy after school, and put an end to the young girl's dream. She was publically humiliated by her mother, who had brought the police and slapped her in front of the boy and grabbed her by her hair, was taken to the police station where she was given a warning and sent home.

Grace sank deeper into her world, hiding her pain and putting on her mask for the outside world.

The '70s was also the year of great political unrest. Black students fed up with policies of the then white-minority rule marched to Soweto, a township in Johannesburg, to protest against the use of the Afrikaans language as the medium of instruction in schools when police fired on them.

Dozens were killed at the time, although the exact number remains unknown.

Soweto Student Uprising

On the morning of June 16, 1976, thousands of students from the African township of Soweto, outside Johannesburg, gathered at their schools to participate in a student-organized protest demonstration. Many of them carried signs that read, 'Down with Afrikaans' and 'Bantu Education – to Hell with it;' others sang freedom songs as the unarmed crowd of schoolchildren marched towards Orlando soccer stadium where a peaceful rally had been planned. The crowd swelled to more than 10,000 students. En route to the stadium, approximately fifty policemen stopped the students and tried to turn them back. At first, the security forces tried unsuccessfully to disperse the students with tear gas and warning shots. Then policemen fired directly into the crowd of demonstrators. Many students responded by running for shelter, while others retaliated by pelting the police with stones.

That day, two students, Hastings Ndlovu, and Hector Pieterson died from police gunfire; hundreds more sustained injuries during the subsequent chaos that engulfed Soweto. The shootings in Soweto sparked a massive uprising that soon spread to more than 100 urban and rural areas throughout South Africa.

The immediate cause for June 16, 1976, march was student opposition to a decree issued by the Bantu Education Department that imposed Afrikaans as the medium of instruction in half the subjects in higher primary (middle school) and secondary school (high school). Since members of the ruling National Party spoke Afrikaans, black students viewed it as the "language of the oppressor." Moreover, lacking fluency in Afrikaans, African teachers and pupils experienced first-hand the negative impact of the new policy in the classroom.

The Soweto uprising came after a decade of relative calm in the resistance movement in the wake of massive government repression in the 1960s. Yet during this "silent decade,' a new sense of resistance had been brewing. In 1969, black students, led by Steve Biko (among others), formed theSouth African Student's Organisation (SASO). Stressing black pride, self-reliance, and psychological liberation, the Black Consciousness Movement in the 1970s became an influential force in the townships, including Soweto. The political context of the 1976 uprisings must also take into account the effects of workers' strikes in Durban in 1973; the liberation of neighboring Angola and Mozambique in 1975; and increases in student enrollment in black schools, which led to the emergence of a new collective youth identity forged by common experiences and grievances (Bonner).

CHAPTER 5

The 80s

There would be many family deaths in the family and Grace would suffer greatly in the coming years. Her Grandfather passed away in Umgeni Road, the same day her eldest niece was born. Grace remembers the day with great sorrow. The year flew by and Grace's home life was not getting any easier. As she got older, the more demanding people around her became. Grace had to learn to cook from the age of nine. She would stand on the chair to reach for the stove to cook for the family as her mother was often late from work. As Grace got older the chores became more and more.

Grace would often question her "special parents" about why she could not tell anyone about them, She wondered why they lived only in the buildings and that they were very quiet whilst Grace was being punished for things that made the family angry and she was often blamed even though Grace told them. They called her a liar and said she made up stories. Grace turned fifteen when she got her first period. She was a late bloomer as she had a tiny body and developed physically very slow.

Grace still went to the church with the neighbors, then to the Hare Krishna temple, sometimes went with her friend, to leave her at Namaaz classes. That year at school, was turbulent, The children rioted and grace and her friends started their own movement. They managed to get students out of classes and boycotted classes. They aimed stink bombs at the teachers and it was chaos for a few days until the police were called in. Grace and her friends were taken in the police vans and let off with a warning.

The headmaster called Grace's parents and asked that she be removed from the school as she was the head of the student movement that was influencing other students not to go to classes. Her parents begged and pleaded but to no avail.

The year was 1981 and her dad bought a black and white television. It was the highlight of the year as this was the first time Grace would see a Fairytale Princess and Prince getting married. Grace started to dream of a life for herself after this magical wedding. The **wedding** of Prince **Charles and Lady Diana** Spencer took place on Wednesday 29 July 1981 at St Paul's Cathedral in London, United Kingdom. … Their **marriage** was widely billed as a "fairytale **wedding**" and the "**wedding** of the century". It was watched by an estimated global TV audience of 750 million people.

And so began her search for a knight in shining armor. Grace kept diaries since she was nine years old and her mother often found them and beat Grace and destroyed her diaries, but Grace still continued to write on whatever piece of paper she could find.

Finally, it was decided that Grace would live with an aunt in another area of Chatsworth. The aunt was a mean lady who kept Grace's clothes in the box under the bed, made Grace sit on the cold floor to eat her food whilst the family sat on the chairs and ate their meals at the dining table. The aunt would make Grace do all the housework and sometimes when she went out visiting, she would leave food outside next to the outside toilet. Grace would often find herself sharing her meals with the birds, Grace longed for a life of peace and tranquility and so found herself immersed in her studies again. Apollo High was known for its high standard of education and Grace worked really hard to keep up with the other students.

One day Grace's mom was visiting and Grace told her that she wanted to go back with her and promised to be good. Grace was packed up and was excited to be going back home to her family. It was on the bus that Grace would meet her future partner.

The next year would bring many hardships for Grace. With the promise of marriage she was duped into sleeping with her partner and as a result, fell pregnant. She was so devastated and with a heavy heart gave back her school books. Her dream to be an archaeologist ended that day.

The families were notified and arrangements were made for them to be married. Her mum bought her a pretty floral dress and lovely sandals. Grace, with her mum and dad, went to the magistrate's court to get her married. As was the custom, they could not be married in the traditional way because of the pregnancy.

The hour came and went, the partner still did not show up, his mother finally shows up with his identity document, saying that he was working in another town and could not make it. So with a huge disgrace and heavy heart, Grace was dragged to her parent's home. That afternoon, Grace was given a severe beating both by her brother and mother for disgracing the family name.

The day went passed with tears, screaming, and shouting at Grace. Lost and forlorn, Grace was thrown out of the house, few clothes packed in a plastic bag, she was told never to return there.

Nowhere to go Grace sat out in the dark, crying and crying. It the neighbour, who took her for the night and he had known Grace's partner, so he made an attempt to get hold of him. The partner took Grace with reluctance to his home and the abuse continued. Grace was physically, emotionally and sexually assaulted daily. It was the final nail on the coffin when the partner brought another woman to share the bed with him and Grace. With sheer strength, Grace threw a lamp at the partner, pulled the woman by the hair and slapped her. Grace pregnant at five months, was kicked and beaten blue by her partner, and chased out of his house.

Taking two buses home, Grace arrived at her parent's, swollen feet, barely breathing and full of tears. Her mother was in the garden, took one look at her, and said" what you want here?" Grace cried and tried to explain, but her mother would not listen to her. In the end, she gave her a glass of water and said Grace should go back to where she came from, that there was no place for her there.

Grace's dad had come out to the garden and called her into the house. He was drunk and started to shout at Grace ' what have you done? I had high hopes for you and you were going to taking us out of poverty He fell on his knees and said' today you killed me' and would those inflicted wounds Grace was sent out again.

Grace sat outside for a long time, not knowing where to go. Another neighbor came to visit and they saw her sitting outside, went to talk to her parents and when they came out, they asked Grace to go with them. Grace would live with the neighbors in another town called Phoenix for the rest of her pregnancy. The family was Christians and they taught Grace how to pray to Jesus and read the bible. Grace was treated with dignity and respect and they gave her love, which for Grace was so special. It was the first time in her almost sixteen years, someone was showing her how to love another person.

Grace gave birth to a beautiful baby girl, and on the day of discharge, her parents and her partner came to collect them. Grace felt a deep disappointment but had no choice where to go next. The drive home was blurred by tears and silence.

Grace, her parents, the partner arrived home in Chatsworth, there was her Aiya. it was an emotional day. but was cut short, when the parent's announced that Grace and her baby would be moving with her partner to a place her mother had found for them.

It was a big fight again when Grace refused to move in with her partner, her Aiya finally looked at Grace, with her tears, she blessed her without a word.

Grace moved in front of her parents' house, in a one-room shared with other people. Grace was sent to work a few days later with her elder sister and her husband. They both worked in a clothing factory in Clairwood and got Grace a job in the cutting room as a quality checker. Grace's mum took care of the baby, whilst Grace worked and paid her mother to look after the baby. In the meantime, her partner was still abusing Grace daily. One morning, while getting ready for work, her partner took a bush knife and held it to her throat. With a force from nowhere, Grace pushed and kicked him. He managed to punch Grace in the face, before she found the strength to grab the baby and run out the room, leaving her partner on the floor, writing in pain, as she kicked him in his private parts.

Grace took her baby to her mother and left for work as usual. Only Grace didn't get on the bus to work, instead, she found herself at the family doctor. After crying and describing events in her life, the young doctor said' Grace, you so intelligent, use your head. Go far away as possible and find yourself work. When you are settled, come and fetch your child'. Grace questioned who would support the baby for milk and nappies? He said ' Don't worry, I will make sure your baby will never go hungry ' and the doctor kept his promise and remained friends to this day.

With a heavy heart, Grace dragged her feet and went up the hill back to her parent's home. Her mother was washing clothes in the bathroom and the baby was asleep in the bedroom downstairs. Grace found her chance, so she sat down and wrote a letter to the baby, packed a few sets of clothes, and sneaked out of the house.

Grace made her way towards the highway, she hitchhiked all the way and ended up in the streets of Johannesburg. A guardian angel was watching over Grace, as her journey was smooth and adventurous. Grace made new friends and was not afraid of the future, in fact, she did not think of tomorrow. Grace did not understand she could not mix with other people of different skin colors. She was so enthralled with her new friends

The first friends were Heather, Cathy, and Ian and they had funny accents, had red hair and freckles, and were quite pale in color. She had come from a country called Scotland.

They were in the park where Grace was 'camping out' and invited her to go to the nightclub with them. Grace didn't know what a nightclub was, so she eagerly followed them. The security refused to let Grace in and her three friends started shouting' we will make all the people leave the club if you do not allow our friend in' So it was then explained to Grace why it was happening. The color of her skin meant she was not allowed in any place that was 'white'. There were signs on the doors of almost every building ' nonwhite only'. Grace had the most special first evening in the big city called Johannesburg. It was a town full of foreign people from all over the world. They had come in search of a rich life.

Grace would have no money, no food, and would end up on the streets begging for a meal. Grace slept under the stars in Joubert Park for two weeks, when she would finally make a breakthrough. Grace was sitting at the station in Joubert Park with her begging bowl, It was on such a fine morning at my usual spot on the train station, begging for a few pennies, when she would meet her Guardian Angel and that would change the course of her life and the future.

John Edward Clayton Smith was a sixty years old European Man when she had the fortune of meeting him that day on the station. He passed her and looked over his shoulder and came towards her again. He dropped a card in her begging cup and handed her 50c and the newspaper. He said to her ' call the number on the card if you need help'.

She didn't sleep much that night but for sure early in the morning she went to the call box and with 50c made the call and seven hours later she would end up on the doorstep of John's offices. Without hesitation, he wanted to hear her story. With total trust for this stranger, Grace began her tale of the life she had from the age of five till he gave her his card the day before.

He listened in total silence and she asked him why did he want to help her? His reply was that he saw her sadness as it was his sadness. The suffering he endured made him turn back to her and rescue her.

John said that he was an orphan and was left on the docks of London. A sailor on leave onshore found him and gave him to some poor people to care for him. He grew up living on the docks, at the age of seven he was shining shoes and selling newspapers. He did odd jobs for the ship's crew and before he knew it, he was fourteen years old. He was fascinated with the ships and he decided to stow away on one of the ships. He stayed hidden till the ship was at sea and he began to wander around the decks. A sailor noticed him and after a severe beating decided to give him odd jobs till the ship anchored at the harbor.

The ship traveled for several months. John didn't recall how long it took to reach the harbor. The ship eventually docked in the Port of

Natal, South Africa. John left the ship and found a place to stay, again doing odd jobs, decided to go to school. He worked during the day and studied at night. He wanted to become a captain of a ship one day, so he studied and worked for many years till he had qualified and got his degree.

He got a job in the electronics field and decided to stay in that field.

John then studied further in engineering and saved enough money to start his own business. It was during this time that he met beautiful Bella, married her, and had two lovely sons, Ian and Mark. The family moved to Johannesburg when the mines were in high demand for workers. He worked there for a period of time and doubled his money. After that success upon success was bestowed on this kind gentleman.

"There are only two ways to live your life. One is as though nothing is a miracle. The other is as though everything is a miracle."

At John's farm, Grace learned how to drive a car, ride horses, and swim. Grace found the library especially fascinating with books on every subject. So began her search for the 'Truth' or 'God' once again. Grace remembers reading a book called 'Many Lives, Many Masters,' and she became intrigued once more with her religion and culture. Grace also learned about apartheid and the 'whites only' policy.

There was a time when Grace was stopped for walking on the street where there were only 'white' people. She was taken in the police van, asked for her identity papers, which she didn't have, they explained to her where to apply for one and left her in the 'nonwhite' area. Grace then became 'Tracey'.

One day in 1985, Mr. Clayton had a business meeting in the city and took Grace along. When they entered the Cafe and sat down, there were loud whispers' kafir lover' and Mr. Clayton was visibly shaken and the crowd started chanting 'kafir lover', another large built 'white' man came towards Grace and threw the bowl of sugar on her head and that's when Mr. Clayton grabbed Grace's hand, pushed aside the crowd and took her to safety. There were many instances when Grace was confronted with the 'whites only' policy but she stood firm and proud. Grace's friends were from all walks of life, different skin colors, different countries, and languages and it fascinated Grace. She was bold and daring. The more rules were enforced, the more she broke them.

Grace lived on the Claytons farm, almost four years. Grace went back after three months of living on the farm to fetch her baby from her family but was turned away. After a few attempts, she got the baby to come with her to Johannesburg. But the baby could not adjust to the climate and got very sick. Grace had no choice but to send the baby back to her parents, with the promise that she would take care of her for the rest of her life financially, to which Grace kept her promise. She brought the baby for the holidays and tried unsuccessfully to keep her permanently. The child was growing up and the family was filling her head with stories of Grace, so the child grew to hate Grace. The family and Grace fought for years over the child and Grace had to let go when the child turned eighteen. Opportunities were given to the child to join the family numerous times, but she chose to be with Grace's parents rather than build a relationship with her own siblings.

During this time Grace turned 21, she had fallen in love for the first time and it was a

'white man'. She had a whirlwind romance and the relationship lasted three years with her having her second son. The new love of her life, had to leave suddenly while Grace was eight months pregnant for her son. The partner returned to his home country and Grace was left to fend for herself once again. Mr. Clayton taught Grace how to save money and told her to see the world while she was young. He would pour over the world maps and point out countries and tell her of the history of the world. So it was that he put her on her first plane ride abroad. It was to visit her second son's grandparents. The trip was to Portugal and they ended up visiting Spain and Italy at the same time.

It was an incredible holiday and Grace was promised marriage again but she was adamant to return to her country South Africa to her family. Grace parted as good friends with the family and kept in touch with everyone for many years until it was time to let go of the past.

Grace went back to work for Mr. Clayon Smith and lived independently for another two years before settling down with the man who would become her husband for the remainder of her life.

CHAPTER 6

The 90s

The end of apartheid was almost over, and Grace and her partner were one of the several mixed couples to get married that year.

Grace and her knight in shining armour finally tied the knot and two weeks later she found out she was pregnant for her third son.

The wedding would last three days and nights and people would talk about the wedding years later. Grace would have her last child, a girl, at the age of twenty-nine and live comfortably for the next few years.

Grace and her husband bought a beautiful house in Croydon and lived for eleven years.

One evening when Grace came from work, she showered and went to the prayer place. she lit the lamp and closed her eyes in prayer. She was very troubled as her youngest daughter, a six-month-old baby, had to go for an eye operation the following week. So instead of praying with her eyes closed, Grace began crying to 'God' begging him to help her as she was helpless, full of work stress, and two other young children to see too.

Suddenly she felt someone touching her hair and rubbing her back along the shoulders. With her eyes still closed, thinking it was her husband, she fell to her knees. That's when she opened her eyes and saw the walls covered in red, and the carpets had mounds of it too. It was kungum. Grace started to shake uncontrollably, She was alone in the prayer room. She half ran, half walked, and screamed for her husband and children. They all came running to see what was happening. Grace had heard and read many of Sai's books and teachings from a young age. But only started to worship Sai at a later age when she got older. She called her mother in Durban, her mother confirmed what Grace was thinking, Sri Sathya Sai Baba had come to the home.

This was nothing so strange as Grace had been talking to her special parents since she was a child.

A week went by and the time for the eye operation began. Grace's husband and she took their baby early that morning and as it was a day clinic, they were able to take her home soon after the operation. Grace was very troubled and anxious as her boss did not give her leave to see her baby. They got home and Grace had to go to work, so she was a little late, and the rest of the day her boss was watching her like a hawk. Grace finally snapped at her and told her, she had enough so she was going home. Grace walked out and went home to her family. The next two months were very stressful, the boss came home and they had a chat and she advised Grace to go to the doctor and take a rest. During that time Grace's extended family visited and being Christians did not believe her when she showed them the prayer place. They said it was demons and that Grace should throw the lamp out. Grace didn't follow their advice and chose to stay away from them.

All Grace knew that day was that she was walking towards the car park at work and suddenly she was searching for her car. The guard came and helped her and showed her where the car was, she felt very stupid and got in the car feeling very strange indeed.

Everything was confusing, She was floating between reality and dream state. Grace drove on the motorway towards home and found herself at the family doctor. The receptionist offered her some tea and made her wait in the waiting room. When it was her turn to see the doctor Grace realized why she was there. The doctor listened then referred her to the clinic saying she was suffering from stress burnout.

The doctor told her that she needed a break from work and was sending her to the hospital to rest. He gave a letter of admission and a sick note for the work. Grace had to leave her husband and children behind to get better. After arranging with the nanny to take care of the children her husband drove her that evening to the hospital.

They drove in silence to Minerva Clinic in Bedfordview, Grace clasped hands tightly, around her body, afraid of the future. The

Clinic had a welcoming appearance, the gardens had a green lawn, colourful flowers in bloom and huge old trees overlooking a huge swimming pool. This looked more like a mansion than a hospital.

Upon entering the building, they were greeted by a nurse then was seen by the psychiatrist. And shown to the room. The room had a single bed, with a bedside table and a night lamp. The curtains were floral coloured and brightened up the dull room. The room overlooked the swimming pool and the beautiful garden.

Grace had to share the room with another patient. That evening she was given a sleeping tablet as she had not slept for a couple of nights. The nurse was a stern lady who never smiled.

The patient on the other side of the room was extremely ill, and barely able to talk. She had visitors, so Grace read a little bit then went to sleep, the tablet doing its work. Early the following morning the patient sharing the room introduced herself and they both became good friends. Her name was Shireen, she was twenty-one years old and of Jewish culture.

Grace was a Hindu, who carried chanting beads, idols and did meditation wherever she was. It was an odd friendship. Shireen was a patient at these hospitals from the early age of eleven as she was an anorexic.

It is an eating disorder when a person's eating habits and relationship with food becomes difficult. Eating problems can disrupt how a person eats food and absorbs nutrients, which affects physical health, but can also be detrimental both emotionally and socially.

There is no single reason why someone may develop an eating disorder - it can be the result of a combination of genetic, psychological, environmental, social, and biological factors. While they can be profoundly serious mental health conditions, they are also treatable and, although it may take a long time, full recovery is possible.

In her grief at the loss of her dad, she blamed herself for her dad dying and therefore stopped eating. She was known by many hospitals, nurses and doctors knew her very well and had given up on Shireen recovering.

Grace was drawn to this young lady and wanted to help her recovery. Grace started to mix with other patients and soon she became their confidante and went around giving hugs and support to others. Forgetting her own reasons for her stay, Grace went around being a protector and pretend nurse. Shireen had many visitors, one being the Rabbi and he seemed pleased to Grace. The patients started to like Grace and sought her out when they needed support or someone to listen to.

Some said they saw a 'halo 'around Grace, a kind of light that shone when she walked past. They did activities during the day in another building. Grace was starting to like being there. Grace thought she was a nurse because everyone used to come to her to talk and ask her to get things for them. A few days later she woke up to strange noises coming from the other side of the room.

Grace got out of bed and went over to Shireen's side of the bed. Shireen was throwing up and a funny smell was coming from her. Grace screamed out for help, and whilst waiting for the nurse to arrive, she rushed to the bathroom, wet the flannel, and wiped Shireen's face. Grace held a sick bowl in front of her and she kept on vomiting. The smell was getting stronger, as Grace lifted the cover of Shireen, she noticed she had soiled herself as well. Shireen was turning blue and Grace kept on screaming for help, as there was no alarm to raise for help in the room.

Grace gave her sips of water and held her tightly in her arms, comforting her. The colour slowly returned to Shireen's face. Grace asked her if she were able to stand and walk to the bathroom and she replied she would try. Grace had no idea where the strength came from, but she managed to half carry, half drag Shireen to the bathroom. she managed to sit on the toilet, and the diarrhoea continued, while Grace stripped the soiled clothes and washed her face and body. The colour on her face was returning to normal, Grace put on clean pyjamas for her and got her back to sit on the bed, while she stripped and changed the bedding. Grace made her comfortable back on her bed, made certain she was alright and then went to make a cup of tea for her.

Grace finally found the nurse and explained to her what had taken place with Shireen and asked for a cup of tea for Shireen. The nurse was so rude, shouted at Grace and told her to mind her own business, that Shireen was on her way out so she should not have bothered helping her. Grace was crying by then, softening slightly she grudgingly made the cup of tea. Grace took it back to Shireen and she slowly sipped every drop of the tea. At breakfast, Grace fed her a few eggs and toast.

Nobody seemed to care for Shireen, all had given up, but Grace refused to let her die. She regained her strength a bit more and spoke clearly to Grace. The vomiting and diarrhoea had stopped. It was about eleven am and the nurses sent Grace to do some activities in another part of the hospital. Grace went very reluctantly as she was still overly concerned about her friend Shireen.

It was while Grace was doing the painting when she heard a voice in her head, someone calling her name. She ran out of painting class, straight to their room. Shireen's bed was stripped clean and there was no sign of Shireen. Grace was devastated, frantically started searching the communal areas for her, Grace had no luck in finding her. Grace was sobbing hysterically and rushed out to the garden and found a spot in the shrubs to hide from everyone.

Time had passed, as she sat and meditated on Shireen's name. The same nurse came looking and found her. She told Grace that Shireen had taken a turn for the worse and they were not expecting her to live. She was transferred to another hospital by ambulance. Grace was so crushed, she bawled her eyes out, shouting that she wanted to see Shireen. The nurses got upset with her behaviour and threatened to sedate her if she did not calm down immediately.

That moment another nurse came and told Grace that there was a call in the public phone booth Grace ran to answer the call and it was Shireen's mum on the line. She told Grace that Shireen was not letting anyone near her and kept on asking for Grace. She told her that she would get permission to visit Shireen. The nurses refused to let Grace go see her, Grace shouted, cried, begged, and pleaded but they bluntly refused. Instead, they called the psychiatrist. He arrived a short while later, after writing a few notes, he referred Grace to another hospital which Grace later found out was a mental institution. Grace then got angry with their decision and screamed for them to call her husband. They brought in her husband an hour later, talked to him about Grace's behaviour and suggested to him that he sign the documents for her transfer. Grace pleaded with her husband and told them that she entered on her own free will and they could not force her to go there.

After an hour of begging and pleading with her husband, he agreed that she should come home instead of being transferred to the mental institution. The psychiatrist looked so mean and angry, he wrote in large letters RHS - refused hospital stay and explained to both of them, that it meant that no hospital would help her if she ever got ill again.

Grace was so relieved to be getting out, she replied that she would never need their help if she lived. She went to the room and hurriedly packed the few pieces of stuff she had brought with her and once outside in the car, she told her husband to drive her to the hospital where Shireen was. He did not hesitate; he was a very patient and understanding husband.

It was a short journey on the motorway to Links field hospital. The building was brown and looked cold and hostile. They arrived at the hospital, down the long, white corridors they walked and, there was Shireen's mum and the Rabbi outside the ward where Shireen was. Her mum told Grace how happy she was to see her, as Shireen was refusing all help from doctors and nurses. She even refused to see the Rabbi, she only asked to see Grace . Grace was concerned that the Rabbi was offended that Shireen asked for her and not him. He just nodded his head to say she could go into the ward. Shireen was in a private ward, as she saw Grace enter, she screamed out her name and tears started to roll from both their eyes.

They both held onto each other tightly, and when she was calm enough, she explained to Grace that she was fed up with hospitals, doctors and life and she did not need them anymore. Grace held her and gently told her that if God wanted her God would take her when it was her time, not before. However, Grace sat with her and prayed for her to get well. Shireen nodded off to sleep. Grace sat quietly praying, while she slept. The Rabbi and her mum came into the ward and Grace asked whether she could have a few more minutes with Shireen which they agreed.

It was a good few minutes later Shireen opened her eyes and told of the dream she had.

In the dream she spoke to her father and that he told her he was sad to see that way and that he wanted her to get better and start a new life. She then asked Grace to pray for her again. Grace asked her if she would now let the doctors help her and she replied yes. Grace called the mum and Rabbi, and both were surprised to see Shireen smiling and laughing. The doctor came in and put a drip on Shireen then Grace said goodbye with a promise to visit the next day.

It was early the next day when Grace received a call from Shireen's mum to say that she was being discharged and would Grace fetch her from hospital.? Shireen was happy to see Grace and they left the hospital together. She wanted to see Grace's children, so Grace took Shireen to her home. Together they phoned Shireen's mum and told her that they would be late as Shireen was having lunch with Grace's family. Shireen played with the children while Grace prepared lunch, and no one watching them together would believe that they both had both been patients at the hospital. Shireen recovered very well, both of them kept in touch for two years and Shireen went on to get married and moved to America to her new life.

Then came Diana the fortune teller, who had predicted Grace's future and years later Grace would recall her words as they came true, one by one. Grace did not know about tarot cards or palm reading. Diana would take Grace under her wing and told her that she was a natural-born healer and that Grace would someday work as a healer.

Diana was an interesting and lively person to be with, they often sat late in the evenings under the skies full of stars, talking about their dreams.

It was about a year later Grace was working for Rosebank Corporate College when she met Karen. She used to phone the college every day looking for work until Grace got her boss to interview her and offer her a job. Karen became Grace's assistant and they soon became close friends. Every day Karen would bring in fresh flowers, happy to be working. As they became friends Karen opened to Grace about her life.

Karen was twenty-five years old when Grace met her. She never had a boyfriend, nor did she have any girlfriends. Grace became her friend she relied on for love and support. You see, Karen had childhood sugar diabetes.

The actual causes of the diabetic condition are little understood, in both children and adults. It is widely speculated that diabetes occurred when inherited genetic characteristics are triggered by environmental factors such as diet or exercise.

She was diagnosed too late. Karen was neglected as a child; her parents were alcoholics and did not pay much attention to her as a child. Karen grew up lonely and unwanted.

Karen's illness was making her lose her hair and teeth. She was becoming bald and losing weight fast. Grace did not know much of the illness back then, however, Grace stood by her as only a best friend could do. Grace supported and gave her love, which she seemed to lack in her young life.

Karen became a regular visitor at Grace's home, and she loved the children. She often brought them gifts. Karen's health started to deteriorate about four months into the friendship. She often fell into a coma and a few times had to be airlifted to hospital. Her nanny would ring first to let Grace know which hospital she was at, so Grace visited every hospital she was admitted to in her short life.

Karen touched Grace's heart as no other person could. She was a gentle and kind, soft-spoken and well-mannered young lady. It broke Grace's heart every time she saw Karen in the hospital. The last time Karen went into a coma for a week, and the doctor told the family there was no hope for her., if she survived, she would be a vegetable - his words.

Grace visited Karen every day for the week, held her hands and spoke to her. Grace still believed she heard her during those visits. Grace got the call a week later to say that Karen was awake and was discharged from the hospital. Grace went around to see her the next day at home and the nanny gave her a message from Karen as she was unable to speak then. She told Grace to listen to Celine Dion - "Because you loved me" and always remember that she loved Grace so much.

Grace cried every time she heard that song because it brings back memories of her darling friend Karen. She died two days later after Grace visited. Karen had requested her body be donated to medical science, so there is a plaque at the local church in her memory.

Grace did not have enough time to process her feelings, as she had another ailing person come into her life. Her young cousin was in the hospital and had just been diagnosed with bone cancer, he was only fourteen at the time. He came from Durban to a specialist hospital in Pretoria. He had a fever, and the operation was postponed so he wanted to come to recuperate at Grace's home. Their bond grew in strength, and he loved Grace so much. He would wait patiently at the gate for Grace to come from work and happily would give a drawing he had done just for her.

He stayed with Grace and her family before and after the operation on his knee where the doctors had found the tumour. Oliver and his mum went back to Durban after staying with them for about six weeks.

Oliver and Grace spoke frequently on the phone. It was not even two weeks before Oliver got ill and was admitted to the hospital again.

Grace rushed down to see him in hospital and that was the last time she would see her young cousin alive.

He was a bright young lad, full of talent and love to share with the world. When Oliver passed away, Grace finally broke down and cried her heart out. Grace became depressed and could not eat or drink. She had sleepless nights and was short-tempered with the children.

She could not understand that grief was a process and she was trying extremely hard to cope with it. It was a day when she was feeling very depressed, and she was at the bus stop crying when an elderly lady approached her and sat beside her. She hugged her when she shared her painful story with the lady. She silently listened and then advised Grace to try volunteering to help others. She took her advice and started to volunteer at Little Eden, a school for special needs children.

CHAPTER 7

Millennium 2000 and the move to Poland

Grace began fervently to worship daily, meditating on Lord Shiva, She often visited her child and parents in Durban or they all came to visit her family in Croydon. Grace had a happy life, until the tragic experience the night of 12th August 2000, one week after her thirty-sixth birthday.

The was an armed home invasion whereby Grace, her husband, and three children were tied and bond, both hands, and feet with metal wires. The family would be tortured for several hours and her husband pistol-whipped. The armed men demanded more cash and jewelry and when they could not find it, they got angrier and Grace told them she knew where the cash and jewelry were and begged them to leave her family.

The men took her to the bedroom, leaving two others to watch over her family with pistols pointed at their heads. Grace opened the safe and when they could not find anything of value, with hesitation the gunman pulled the trigger.

The bullet missed her head by inches, and Grace left her body, where she came face to face with the Lord Jesus Christ. Grace's spirit hovered over the room from above, she watched the four men take turns to violently sexually assault her tiny body.

It was a few minutes where she experienced heaven and was sent back into her physical body. The robbers left soon after the rape of Grace, taking all appliances, including the vehicle as a getaway. It took several hours before the family was able to summon help. It was only the following morning that Grace was taken to the hospital by her 'white' friend to get medical assistance for her ordeal. South Africa was very much still a 'white' country and it was difficult to get the help she needed urgently.

Her friend paid for the treatment and Grace was given a course of anti-HIV treatment for nine months. The next few months would be a spiritual fight between Christianity and Hinduism. Grace got a ticket to Australia for her 36th birthday and because of the incident, it lay forgotten until Grace made the decision to get away from everything for a holiday. That Christmas of the year 2000, was when Grace finally began to heal from within.

The decision to leave South Africa was Grace's alone and so began their immigration process.

They arrived in Europe on 2nd August 2001, the home of her husband's family in Poland.

Life was very difficult for Grace and the three children. Her husband had to go back to South Africa to sell the property and the vehicle and business the family-owned. It would take him five years to join the family in Poland. In the meantime, Grace and the children struggled with harsh winters, no friends and family, language barrier, and many other complications. The community did not accept them very well, as they were the first nonwhite family in the village so they stood out in the crowd. The children were subject of racial attacks at school, often beaten and bullied. Grace was called ugly names and spat upon, but she taught her children to be resilient and patient. The children had tutors to cope with school life, and Grace learned from tv to understand the language. It was one of the neighbors who finally approached and asked Grace to help with the English lesson for her daughter. That's when the reputation grew and then there were sixteen children coming t the home and that's when Grace decided on getting another premise to run the school.

There she would go on to open a language school and build a reputation and the school was a success.

Grace continued to do volunteer work at the school for Special Needs Children, and she felt this was her calling to work with sick people and underprivileged children. She became a volunteer and a health care worker for both children and the elderly. She loves her work with absolute passion.

She became popular in the village as her reputation spread about the work she was doing both as a teacher and volunteer. Grace was invited by the South African Embassy in Warsaw, Poland to become a member of the Polish/South African Cultural committee. Grace would appear in the local newspaper and be well respected in the community.

CHAPTER 8

October 2004

Grace called her parents in Durban, to tell them of the dream she had the night before. She spoke to her dad for over an hour. They discussed a lot of things about his coming birthday in November, and she told him of her plans to come for Christmas to spend with him and the family.

That day after that call Grace was very anxious and disturbed. She couldn't think of anything except memories of her dad flashed through her mind. The next day being Saturday she got up early and called her parents again, her dad picked up the phone and spoke to all three of the children. Grace didn't know that was going to be the last time that they would see him again. Grace sent her oldest son to the shops to buy a gift for her third son, as his birthday was coming up in a few days. For some reason, Grace decided to have a small party for him on Saturday, instead of waiting for his birthday on Wednesday the following week.

That evening they spent time at her in-law's house. .All she did was talk about her father and share with them memories of her childhood. They left them quite late in the night and returned to her home. Grace tossed and turned the whole night, restless and worried.

Early the next morning, it being Sunday 3rd October 2004, the first thing Grace did was take her mobile phone to send a text to her eldest daughter, who still lived with her parents. While she was texting the house phone rang. It was 6.30 am and Grace will never forget that phone call. All she heard was crying and in between the sobs, her daughter told her that her dad was taken to the hospital at 3 am and was serious.

Grace quickly put the phone down, rushed to wake the rest of the children, and told them that she had to go to South Africa, her dad was in the hospital.

Next, she phoned her sister-in-law and told her that she was going to South Africa and would she take care of the children?. She immediately came home while Grace packed a few clothes hurriedly, got dressed, and said goodbye to the children. Her sister-in-law's son drove Grace to the airport. While on the way Grace just sobbed and prayed to her dad to hold on for her, Grace was on her way to him. It was 110km away from the airport and he drove at high speed to get Grace to the airport on time. As they neared the airport she checked her phone, and there over fifteen messages. She just read one or two of them, made a call, and told the family she was near the airport and would be there the next morning. They arrived at the airport and rushed to the desk, and pleaded with them to get her on the next flight to Durban, South Africa. As she waited for them to sort out her ticket, she felt a sharp pain in her chest, it was like a heart attack. With tears, she stumbled and someone got a chair for her to sit. The desk clerk gave her the ticket and said it was the last place on the plane.

She radioed the security to let her through as it was an emergency, they let her through without checking her bags. She ran to the waiting area to board the plane and there it was announced there was a delay and the plane was leaving in the next half hour. There she sat and chanted, it was to her father in her head she had a conversation, asking him to hold on for her, with tears rolling down her cheeks she managed to board the plane. She sat next to a man who was on his way to see his family in Austria. He asked her why she was crying and she told him that her dad was critical in hospital and that she was on the way to see him in hospital.

He then told her of his experience with his dad. " It was Christmas and I was flying from America to see my parents in Austria. At the airport, I phoned my father to arrange to pick me up. My mother answered the phone and passed on the message that my dad had passed away that morning. I broke down right there at the airport. But don't worry Your dad will be waiting for you". They both fell silent for a while.

The steward was passing and Grace requested a vegetarian meal. She replied that since she was on an emergency, flight, that there was no food booked for her. She would organize a sandwich for Grace later. Grace thanked her and continued her silent meditation with her dad.

It was as she was serving the meal, Grace could hear her say to the passengers in the rows behind her that there were no meat or chicken left and that there were only vegetarian meals served. When she came to Grace, she smiled and handed her the vegetarian meal. That was the first meal Grace had since 6.30 am that Sunday morning.

The plane landed at Frankfurt airport, for the changeover. Grace hurriedly got to the payphone and called home to South Africa. Her sister-in-law picked up the phone.

She hesitantly told Grace, her dad was waiting for her, and that he showed signs that he understood that Grace was on the way to him. Grace told her not to lie, she then said, he passed away. Grace dropped the phone and collapsed, people came running to her assistance and she told them what she just heard. Someone brought her water and she got up with tears still rolling down her cheeks, she boarded the next plane to South Africa.

Throughout the journey Grace prayed and chanted, she did not sleep at all that night, the journey was long and her heart was tearing into a million pieces.

She landed in Johannesburg early Monday morning. Her husband was there to meet her, and they took separate flights to Durban. As her ticket was booked from Poland, they had different times to fly. She arrived at Durban international airport, at 8.30 am. Grace went and got a large bouquet of proteas, and waited outside for transport. As she was about to get in the taxi, her brother, and her cousin pulled up and she got into the car.

They drove into Chatsworth in silence, and got to the driveway of her parent's house. They parked the car on the next driveway, as the hearse was reversing down the driveway.

She ran out of the car and raced up the driveway, to the house, and entered the lounge, to see the coffin and the priest doing the prayer.

Mother screamed and shouted out, " You here, your father said to me, not to put him in the freezer when he dies, that I must wait for Grace to come before you bury me"

She then said " you brought your child with you, you didn't wait in the fridge for long"

Everyone was in tears by then, the priest couldn't finish the prayer because Grace insisted on seeing her daddy for the last time.

The day was surreal, Grace was in a dream with her daddy. She couldn't cry anymore, just talked to him and hugged him whilst he lay still and cold. The funeral procession took place, with the ceremonial prayer, and then they took her dad to his resting place. Grace chose not to go to the cemetery, instead, she stayed with her mother and held her tightly for a long time. Somebody asked for something and mother said it was in daddy's cupboard could Grace bring it to her. Grace went upstairs with her eldest daughter and she entered the bedroom and opened the cupboard with the key mother had given her.

There neatly on the shelf was a bundle of folded papers. Grace picked it up and sat on the bed with it. As she opened it, a photo of Grace, as a young girl of fifteen, fell down. Grace picked it up and as she was about to put it away, she opened the folded papers. It was her entire school report neatly arranged in date order. Grace wept and wept, it broke her heart to realize that her daddy loved her so much and was so proud of her.

Grace stayed with her mother for three days before she returned to her children in Poland.

Her children had a story to tell her too. The night daddy passed away, he came to the three children. Her eldest son told her " We were all in bed, I was in my bedroom when I saw someone standing near my bed, I looked and there was father, he stayed for a few minutes and disappeared. I got out of bed and went to go and check on the others and I heard them shout out in their sleep - Don't go, father"

Her daddy came to say his goodbye to her children and blessed them with his presence.

It was on the sixteen-day ceremony- when Grace got up early in the morning. Cooked the food and told the children to write letters to her daddy and place it by the candle and dad's photo in the lounge. When they left for school she went to the lounge and the wooden calendar had turned black with smoke from the candle.

Grace phoned home to her mum immediately and she said they were doing havan prayers, could Grace call back.? Before she put the phone down she said" We doing havan prayers for your father but he came to you "

With her heart heavy, she continued to do the prayer for her daddy. It was while she was praying that God took her on the astral plane, Grace swore secrecy never to reveal what God had shown her. When she opened her eyes, she was flat on the floor. She stood up and drank the milk and turmeric water.

Then she heard banging on the door, and dogs barking. She went to the door and there stood her son. He said he was knocking and ringing the bell for over twenty minutes. Grace apologized and told him she fell off to sleep.

She started to tell him of the dream, but somehow her tongue got tied, she started mumbling words and started shaking. Then a voice said " you must not tell anyone "

Grace drank milk immediately and changed the subject with her son. Then the next few months would be full of grief and sorrow for Grace. She couldn't understand what God wanted her to do, she was so afraid to tell anyone. So she kept this story to herself.

She wrote it in her journals and continued with her work and taking care of the children. It wasn't until she was cleaning her handbag she found the plane ticket and it was exactly the time that dad had passed away when she had that sharp pain at the airport.

CHAPTER 9

In 2006 Grace's husband had finally joined them in Poland, to live with them as a family. Grace and the children had lived for almost five years alone in a strange country while he lived and worked in Johannesburg. Her husband couldn't find a job in Poland, so Grace put his cv online, and a company in England contacted him. He was interviewed by a conference call and was successful.

England 2007

Her husband left for England in March 2007, Grace and the children followed him on June 21st 2007 to Horsham, West Sussex.

It is a beautiful town which has a history from 1066. One of the King's wives came from the town, Her name was Cathrine Howard. Her home is called Chesworth House and is at the edge of town.

Horsham, the name could either mean "horse home", or "Horsa's home". Horsa was a Saxon warrior who was granted land in this area. Horsham's first historical mention was in 947 CE, it was also mentioned in the Doomsday Book in 1086 as a large village, and by the 13th century had grown into a small town.

Initially, Horsham was famous for its horses, but as time went on the town's main trade switched to tanning leather and brewing beer, and by the 16th century, the town boasted 5 separate brewers.

In 1801, Horsham had a population of just 1,539. This grew rapidly and by 1851 there were almost 6,000 people living here, 10,000 in 1900, and now there are around 60,000 people calling themselves Horshamites.

The centre of Horsham is known as the Carfax, a name most likely of Norman origin, meaning 'Quatre Voies' (four ways) or 'Carrefour', a place where four roads meet. As some people may remember, the Carfax once consisted of two concentric ring roads. A redevelopment project in 1992 aimed to reduce traffic around the town centre and to achieve this much of the Carfax and West Street was pedestrianised and a new town square was created.

The main shopping area, Swan Walk, was opened in 1976 and takes its name from the Swan Inn, which once stood where the pedestrian entrance opens onto West Street. In 1989, Swan Walk was enclosed with a glass roof and a bronze swan statue was erected to honour its name.

Not everything has changed though, the Parish Church of St. Mary the Virgin is the oldest building in Horsham and has been in continuous use for nearly eight centuries. It is located at the end of the Causeway, one of the most picturesque and undisturbed areas of the town

Horsham's claim to royalty fame is that Catherine Howard, the fifth wife of Henry VIII lived here. Catherine was born in 1523 and married Henry at the age of 17, but was beheaded just nineteen months later, in 1542, for adultery.

On a lighter note, English comedian, Harry Enfield attended Collyer's sixth form college in Horsham. One of his most famous characters, Kevin the Teenager, even makes mention of living on Merryfield Drive in Horsham.

But by far the town's greatest claim to fame is that Percy Bysshe Shelley was born in Field Place in Broadbridge Heath on 4 August 1792. To celebrate the bicentennial of the romantic poet's birth, the Shelley memorial fountain, known as the "Rising Universe" was erected in 1992. Unfortunately, after various periods of deactivation, it was eventually removed in June 2016 due to the need to reduce spending.

How could we fail to mention that famous actor Michael Caine began his acting career here at the age of 20? Caine responded to an advertisement in The Stage for an assistant stage manager, during his stay he also performed small walk-on parts for the Horsham-based Westminster Repertory Company performing at the Carfax Electric Theatre.

Horsham holds the UK record for the heaviest hailstone ever to fall. On 5 September 1958, a hailstone weighing 140g (4.9 oz) landed in the town. Similar in size to a tennis ball, the impact speed has been calculated at about 100 m/s or 224 mph.

Horsham was also the site of the world's first revolutionary gaol (jail), built-in 1775. You can see the original windows, door, padlock, and keys from the gaol, and experience what a typical cell would have looked like at the Horsham Museum. You'll also find arts and craft galleries, a gallery dedicated to local poetry legend, Shelley, and other fascinating exhibitions from Horsham and around the world.

Grace started to work as a volunteer at the centre for the elderly and would meet the first Royal family. She had tea with the Duke of Kent, the Queen's first cousin. He was with the Mayor of Horsham and the priest of St Mary's Catholic Church

Grace had been a Royal fan of Princess Diana ever since she saw her wedding on the black and white tv screen when she was sixteen years old. Since then she has been collecting articles, books etc on Princess Diana and the Royal family.

Fascinated by history and to find out that Grace lives at Tudor house is another part of history that she lovingly shares with her readers.

It was in 2012 that Grace wrote to the Queen to wish her for the Golden Jubilee celebrations and she received an email and letter from Buckingham Palace. She started to get memories of a past life again. She went back to her royal collection and read the inscription in the William Shakespeare sonnets and then she finally understood that she have lived before.

It has always been her dream to become an archaeologist, but she never got the opportunity. , so instead she travelled a lot and saw over fourteen countries visiting archaeological sites and took thousands of photos of these sites.

She became fascinated with the culture and history of our ancestors. She continued her service to Lord Siva by doing Meditation and doing Raja Yoga.

CHAPTER 10

July 2010

Grace felt that divinity within her and God appeared to her once again. The family thought her behavior was very odd, so she ended up in the hospital.

At the hospital, she was going around taking care of other patients.

One morning she sat out in the garden doing meditation, She sat on the cold cement path, picked up a handful of pebbles, and started chanting, When Grace opened her eyes, the sun was shining gloriously on her face, and as she was about to throw the pebbles away, She realized it was all soft and had grown smaller. Curious she bit into it and it tasted like kadla (chickpeas), Grace was astounded and amazed at what happened. she told no one about this as it would mean that she would be kept longer there.

The visions and her dreams of her Aiya and her late dad began to play on her mind.

There was more to the visions and dreams and she started to research further on her ancestors. There were many signs that her ancestors were trying to send her a message. Grace went back to studying Buddhism, Lord Krishna, and back to reading the scriptures again.

It was during this time that Grace wrote to the Queen and received a Thank you letter from Buckingham Palace. Grace had it framed and it sits on the mantelpiece in her home.

Grace was never into politics but soon realized that it was part of her ancestors and her history. As Grace loved the history of the world, her own history needed to share first before realizing that her ancestors led a far more interesting life than hers.

As Grace grew up in Apartheid South Africa, travelled to many countries and finally settled in Britain, she knew that this was her destiny to uncover the past.

It all started with following the tales of Mahatma Gandhi in his own words.

Satyagraha (1906 -1914)

" The energies of South African Indians, mobilised in the 1890s against growing anti-Indianism in various parts of South Africa, were channelled into a concerted movement, which aimed at eradicating the various disabilities from which Indians of all castes, classes and creeds suffered.

Gandhi, the man at the centre of the movement, explained Satyagraha as 'Soul force, pure and simple ' a weapon for those in search of truth. The defiant spirit of the Empire Theatre mass meeting reflected the commitment of the Indians, who took Gandhi's message to heart. However, they were quick to learn the complexity of the man and his message. 1908

the compromise was interpreted by one person as a betrayal of the original commitment, and he almost killed Gandhi. The agonies of doubt and failure, and indeed the sense of achievement, which speaks of the progress of the campaign from the time it was resumed in June 1908 until its final conclusion in 1914.

Although Gandhi labelled the 1914 Smuts-Gandhi Agreement as a 'Magna Charta,' he recognised that it provided no more than a 'breathing space' from which greater freedom had to flow. So much was clear, however, an era, inedibly linked with the name of the one man had ended. The new era had of necessity to plot its politics, draw up its programs, establish its priorities and enunciate its philosophies minus the presence, the pen, and the mind of Mohandas Karamchand Gandhi.

Grace was stunned to learn so much of her culture and ancestors as she was not taught that in her school history. The history textbooks do not reflect the deeds, words, and actions of the great Indian leader, who later became friends with Nelson Mandela who would end up in prison for 27 years and become the first Black President in South Africa marked the era of apartheid.

Grace learned of the 1949 riots from her dad one day when Grace asked him about his life. There are a few special holidays where Grace and her dad spent hours talking about his life with his parents and his band days..

The Durban Riots 1949

In January 1949, a bitter racial conflict occurred in Durban. The consequent loss of life and property was officially given as follows: deaths (87 Africans, 50 Indians, 1 white, and 4 others whose identity could not be determined), injured (541 Africans, 503 Indians, 11 coloreds, and 32 whites, of the injured 5 died) Buildings destroyed, 1 factory, 58 stores, and 247 dwellings, buildings damaged: 2 factories, 652 stores, and 1285 dwellings.

The Indians of Durban are still bewildered and stunned by the convulsion two weeks ago-one fierce burst of terror which lasted from Friday afternoon, January 14, to Saturday morning, January 15. But let this be clearly understood: this was no race riot, it was no clash between races, there were no pitched battles, no organized assaults, and reprisals by two race groups. The Indians did not fight back. When violence descended on their person, they took cover and remained undercover, from where they were later hounded out, and killed, or burnt inside their homes.

Subsequently, however, cases were reported where some Indians attempted reprisals, but they were quickly dealt with. At no stage, therefore, can the convulsion really be called a race riot.

Briefly, this is what happened. On Thursday evening (January, 13) Indians in the heart of the Indian area were set upon by Africans. They did not know what was happening. On the first day there was hardly any destruction of property, and after some hours, the tide of violence died down.

But at midday on Friday a veritable human cyclone hit the Indian business area. Hordes of Africans, armed with a varied assortment of improvised weapons, swooped down on the Indian People and destroyed both the property and the people in their wake. Looting followed and the whole grim episode took on a positive aspect- the African had something material to gain. The convulsion has taken on a sinister aspect for, despite the efforts of the police, and egged on by many Europeans (who subsequently joined in the looting), the Africans discovered that their reign of terror could have a positive enriching value. They set to it with barbarous determination. The forces of law and order stood by, almost helpless it seemed, as the Africans swept forward in their savage march, and the terror immediately spread to the peri-urban areas, where the outburst of the previous evening became an orgy of murder, arson, rape, and looting which did not seem altogether without aim, purpose, and direction.

The storm burst with unbridled fury on the people who, in the main, lived almost in the same conditions as the Africans who attacked them. The Ilanga Lase Natal, Natal's leading African newspaper, blamed the Indians bitterly, for, it says ' the whole grim business was logical, simply inevitable.' It then advances the following reasons for the convulsion: black marketeering by Indians, Indian opposition to the economic expansion of the African, ' shacketeering' by Indian landlords, social and racial humiliations of Africans by Indians, and the differential treatment of Indians by Europeans which gives the Indians'not only better rights, but a sense of snobbishness and superiority over the Africans.'m

Why?

But if these were the real cause of convulsions, why the senseless massacre of the poor Indians living side by side with the Africans on the perimeter of the city? Why the orgy of violence and rape against defenseless women and children? Was not the destruction and the subsequent looting of Indian business in Grey, Victoria, and Queen street sufficient?

CHAPTER 11

Leaving Politics to the politicians to correct the injustices of the past, Grace continues in her struggles to find the missing pieces that tear her heartstrings.

'What then is Truth ?'

A difficult question, but I have solved it for myself by saying that it is what the voice within tells you. How, then, you ask, different people think of different and contrary truths? Well, seeing that the human mind works through innumerable media and that the evolution of the human mind is not the same for all, it follows that what may be the truth for one may be an untruth for another, and hence those who have made these experiments have come to the conclusion that there are certain conditions to be observed in making those experiments. Just as for conducting scientific experiments there is an indispensable scientific course of instruction, in the same way, strict preliminary discipline is necessary to qualify a person to make experiments in the spiritual realm. Everyone should, therefore, realize his limitations before he speaks of his Inner Voice. Therefore we have the belief based upon experience, that those who would make individual God, must go through several vows, as for instance, the vow of truth, the vow of Brahmacharya (purity) – for you cannot possibly divide your love for Truth and God with anything else–the vow of non-violence, of poverty and non possession. Unless you impose on yourselves the five vows you may not embark on the experiment at all. There are several other conditions prescribed, but I must not take you through all of them. Suffice it to say that those who have made these experiments know that it is not proper for everyone to claim to hear the voice of conscience, and it is because we have at the present moment everybody claiming the right of conscience without going through any discipline whatsoever and there is so much untruth being delivered to a bewildered world, all that I can, in true humility, present to you is that truth is not to be found by anybody who has not got an abundant sense of humility. If you would swim on the bosom of the ocean of Truth you must reduce yourself to a zero. Further than this, I cannot go along this fascinating path.

I have not seen Him, neither have I known Him. I have made the world's faith in God my own, and as my faith is ineffaceable, I regard that faith as amounting to experience. However, as it may be said that to describe faith as experience is to tamper with truth, it may perhaps be more correct to say that I have no word for characterizing my belief in God.

Hinduism allows absolute freedom to the rational mind. It does not demand any undue restraint upon the freedom of human reason, feeling, thought and will. The religious hospitality of Hinduism is provibilant. Its fundamental feature is that it is liberal and catholic. It respects all religions and does not repel any.

The true Hindu eschews no path nor does he condemn any form of spiritual search. He sees no hostility between his creed and the fundamental tenets of other religions. There is no distinction between validity, authenticity and the inspirational character of his faith and other great faiths of the world. A characteristic of Hinduism is its receptivity and all comprehensiveness. It is the religion of humanity and has no difficulty in including other religions in its all-embracing arms and ever-widening field.

The strength of Hinduism lies in its infinite adaptability to the infinite diversity of the human abstract side suited to the metaphysical philosopher; its practical and concrete side suited to the man of peace and seclusion. This has been the Hindu outlook and conviction throughout the ages.

The Vedas are the eternal truths revealed by God to the ancient seers of India. They are the ultimate source to which all religious knowledge could be traced. It consists of three parts:

Philosophy is the essence of religion and sets forth its fundamental doctrines of tenets, the goal and the means of attaining it.

The ritual consists of ceremonials and gives a concrete form to philosophy so that all may understand it.

Mythology explains and illustrates philosophy by means of the legendary lives of great men and supernatural beings.

One can grasp the subtle, philosophical truths by means of such myths. The object of myths and legends is to lure the mind to the truths of religion. Mythology moulds one's character leading to divine life. Despite all differences in metaphysical doctrines, modes of religious discipline and forms of ritualistic practise, there is an essential uniformity in the concept of religion and the outlook of life.

The unity of Hinduism is not of an unchanging creed or a doctrine but it is the unity of a continuously changing life. Religion to a Hindu is an experience or attitude of mind, a consciousness of ultimate Reality, not a theory about God. It is the intuition of Reality, insight into truth, contact with the Supreme and direct apprehension of Reality. The emphasis is on experience as distinct from dogmatism and blind faith. Man becomes aware of God through experience.

Vedic knowledge was experienced by the Rishis. It was heard, not created by human authors. It is spiritual discovery, not creation. Hindus believe in the superiority of intuition to intellectual reasoning. The Vedas are more a record than an interpretation of religious experience.

Hinduism is neither asceticism nor illusionism, neither polytheism nor pantheism. It is the synthesis of all types of religious experience. It is characterised by wide tolerance and deep humanity. Its spiritual purpose is lofty and it is free from all kinds of fanaticism. It is extremely catholic, liberal, tolerant and elastic. It is very stern and rigid regarding fundamentals. It stands unrivalled in the depth and grandeur of its philosophy. Its ethical teachings are lofty, unique and sublime. The various aspects of the one ultimate reality is erroneously referred to as Gods and Goddesses.

It is based on the principle of Reincarnation.- the idea of indestructibility of the soul which goes through the cycles of birth and death until purified to achieve communion with God. Thousands of years ago, our Rishis (Sages) enunciated four paths to God Realisation. That is Karma Yoga, Bhakti Yoga, Jnana Yoga and Raja Yoga. The first two paths are for those who are a slave to their senses and the last two for those who can make the necessary sacrifice of renunciation and meditate to control their senses.

The Supreme Being who is Omnipresent, Omnipotent and Omniscient has given only one sign of his presence that is Creation, Preservation and Dissolution.

CHAPTER 12

The Hindu Trinity is represented by Lord Brahma(Creator) Lord Vishnu(Lord Narayana, the Preserver) and Lord Siva (Rudra, the Destroyer and Reproducer of life)

There is in Hinduism but one God - the Absolute. This God is formless, yet contains all forms; it is invisible, yet seen everywhere; it cannot be heard yet it is in every sound; it has no name yet it is contained in the mystic sound of OM;

A sound incorporating all sounds. Hinduism has created a hierarchy of Gods who represent the various aspects of the absolute. Over the centuries, this hierarchy has crystalised itself into a strict order and has remained essentially the same for nearly 2000 years.

Lord Vishnu

Vishnu, in his many forms and incarnations, is the most widely worshipped of the Hindu Gods. He is the all pervading and omnipresent protector of the universe. Garuda, the eagle (acknowledged as the king of the birds) and sometimes represented as half man and half bird, is the destroyer of evil, symbolised by his traditional enemy, the serpent God, serves as a vahana of the Lord. It is regarded as an apt carrier because of his ability to fly at unlimited speed .

Lord Siva

Siva (literally means auspicious) is generally represented as an ascetic sitting on a tiger man. Snakes are coiled around his body. He has a third eye in the centre of his forehead and a crescent moon rests on his head. His abode is Mt Kalasa. He is also worshipped in the form , Linga, representing the power behind creation.

Seal discovered in the Indus Valley During excavation, has drawn attention as a possible representation of a "yogi" or "proto-Shiva" figure.

Lord Ganesha or Vinayaga

Ganesha, the son of Siva and Parvathy, is the household deity of prudence and prosperity. Legend has it that Ganesha was installed as a sentinel at the door while Parvathy was bathing. Siva, on being prevented from entering, flew into a rage and beheaded Ganesha. Parvathy wept bitterly and pleaded with Siva to give back her son. Siva beheaded the first object he met, that is an elephant and replaced Ganesha's head with an elephant's head.

The trunk of this elephant- headed deity symbolises strength and the head,wisdom. He rides on a rat (mushaka) symbolising agriculture. As rats destroy the corn in the fields, he exerts a protective influence. The deity's protuberant belly symbolises the storehouse and his ears, the supra (winnowing basket) The single tusk represents the piece of iron in a plough which turns the furrow.

The great Epic, The Mahabharatha, is said to have been written by this deity and dictated by the sage Vyasa, on Mount Meru.

Lord Rama

Lord Rama is the seventh incarnation of Lord Vishnu. His exploits form the subject of the great epic, The Ramayana. He was born in Ayodhya (Uttar Pradesh) and was heir to the throne. He was exiled from his kingdom for fourteen years by his father, King Dhasaratha to satisfy the pleas of one of his wives who was desirous that her son, Bharatha inherit the throne.

His devoted wife, Sita, and his brother, Lakshmanna accompanied him into exile into the forest of Dandaka (S.India) Ravana, the ten - headed demon who was the King of Lanka (Ceylon) abducted Sita during her husband's absence. Rama set out in search of her and when he found her in Lanka, a great battle ensued between him and Ravana. Assisted by the monkey chief, Hanuman and Sugriv, he was victorious and brought Sita back to his capital where there was great rejoicing. His brother, Bharatha, who had loyally ruled the kingdom during his absence, welcomed his brother who was now the crowned king. For Hindus Rama is the embodiment of the ideal man and Sita the ideal woman.

Rama is the Supreme ideal of the man of Dharma, dutifulness and discipline. As a son, he was dutiful; as a husband, faithful; as a brother, loyal and as a king, just. The noblest lesson enshrined in the Ramayana is the supreme importance of righteousness in the life of every human being. One must be imbued with a deep sense of conviction about the supremacy of moral principles, ethical values and spiritual ideals. This is the mission and message of his life on earth.

Lord Krishna

Lord Krishna was born near Mathura on the outskirts of Delhi. He is the veritable personification of Love. It is said that whenever injustice and intolerance became rampant, the Supreme Lord Vishnu would descend to earth in the form of an Avatar or incarnation to restore the balance between good and evil. This bodily manifestations or re-incarnations of God are shining illustrations of the upward ascent of the soul. The Avatar is the bridge between morality and immorality.. In an Avatar, the divine and human elements are inextricably blended.

So it came to pass that towards the close of the Dvapara Yuga just over 5000 years ago, a race of demons sprung up and established a reign of terror. One such Incarnation was Krishna and it was at this time that he was born to Devika, the virtuous wife of Vasudeva. He entered this world in one of his darkest hours and helped to spread righteousness. One the very night of his birth, his parents had remove him to a spot, where he was reared by the Yadhavas (cowheads) beyond the reach of his uncle, the notorious Kamsawho sought his life because was warned by a voice from heaven that this son of Devaka would be the cause of his destruction.

As he grew up, he was actively engaged in assisting and advising the Pandavas before and during the war with the Kauravas-known as the Mahabharatha. It was in this capacity as charioteer to Arjuna in that war that he enunciated the purpose of life in the form of the " Song Celestial" or Bhagvad Gita. The teachings by him to Arjuna on the field of battle, graphically described in this book, reveals him as the greatest philosopher of all ages and a Yogi of the highest order.

His whole life recorded in the Bhagavatam was a practical application of his own teachings. In order to know him and to understand the Gita. He was the eight incarnation of Vishnu. He grew to manhood among the cowherds and his love of the gopis (milk-maids) symbolises the yearning of the human soul, for the pleasures of kinship with God. He is usually represented pictorially as a handsome youth playing a flute.

His Avatar had combined in his divine personality the three aspects of creation, preservation and destruction to demonstrate to the world the oneness of the Cosmic Deity. He accomplished the main objective of his incarnation that is to punish the wicked and help the virtuous.

Lord Hanuman

Lord Hanuman is believed to be the eleventh incarnation of Lord Shiva. He is the symbol of Shakti or a bodily manifestation of the power of God. He holds an exalted position in the Hindu Pantheon. He is a deity endowed with muscular strength and his physical feats are recounted in the Ramayana. It is this physical strength and agility that made him an invaluable ally to Rama.

As he was the son of Vahu (Wind God) and Anjini, he could not only fly at the speed of wind, but had the strength to uproot trees and mountains. He could also alter his size at will and even make himself invisible. With his flaming tail, Hanuman reduced Ravana's capital (Lanka) to ashes and returned to Rama.

Shaivism, the philosophy based on the teachings of **Lord Shiva,** is the blend of two lines of development, the Aryan or Vedic and the pre Aryan. Much more than the urbane cult of Lord Vishnu, it has exhibited a close alliance with Yoga. It is not a single cult but a federation of allied cults. The characteristics of shaivism are the exaltation of Siva above all the other Gods, the highly concrete conception of the deity and the intensely personal nature of the relation between him and his devotees.

The discovery of several prehistoric relics of a phallic character, from various parts of India including the chalcolithic sites of Mohenjo-daro and Harappa, shows that the phallic cult with which Saivism is closely associated was a widespread cult in pre vedic India.

Siva is the God of the Yogis, the one who helps man to conquer his lower nature and rise above it into his divine nature. To make this transition, the mind must first be mastered. The mind is said to be related to the moon and, it is believed, that there is an astronomically favourable time when the moon is right for success in man's efforts to transcend his mind.

Siva the Supreme, ultimate Reality is the omniscient, omnipotent and omnipresent. Through his Shakti or power, he causes the material world to come into existence. All the problems of the world are caused by the impure state of the soul which is covered by Mala or Anava which causes the soul to become unaware of its inherent, latent purity and spirituality.

The remedy for all ills lies to the liberation of the Soul.

Siva stands for universal welfare which can only be attained by adhering to the principles of Dharma. Nandi, the sacred Bull of Siva acts as his vahana.

The sanskrit word "Vahana" or vehicle is used for the animals, birds and man who serve as the carriers of the Gods in Hindu mythology. The sacred images of Nandi faces the Linga, in all Siva temples. The worshiper first touches his hands and then bows to the Linga. Nandi is a white bull symbolic of virtue. His four legs represent the four main principles of Dharma or religious duty that is austerity, purity, mercy and charity.

The Constorts of the Hindu Trinity

Saraswathi, the consort of Brahma is the Goddess of Learning, the Arts and Sciences. She is represented as draped in spotless white and sitting on the lotus. The swan is her mount (vahana) and she holds a veena in one hand. She is cosmic intelligence and consciousness and worship of this deity is necessary for purification of intelligence, cultivation of right discernment and Self-Realisation.

In one of her hands she holds the Holy Book embodying the theory of Brahma Nyana (wisdom) and in another, the spotless mala (rosary) symbolises that through Japa and meditation one can attain the highest Para Nyana (Transcendental Wisdom) She is the Pravana Rupini and is called by an endearing name, Veena Vani, as she is the origin of all articulated sounds.

Lakshmi, the consort of Vishnu, rose from the foam of the ocean. She stands on the lotus and is the much sought after Goddess of wealth and prosperity. She does not merely symbolise material wealth as all kinds of prosperity, divine joy, nobility, auspiciousness and benevolence come through her grace. She is worshipped as the Eightfold-Laksmi

The significance of Shakti (Devi) Worship

The name "Devi" is synonymous with Shakti or the Divine Power that manifests, sustains and transforms the universe. The worship of Devi or the Divine Mother is neither sectarian nor belongs to any cult. By Shakti we mean the presupposition of all forms of existential power- the power of knowledge, of sustenance and of omniscience.

God has created this world through Shristi Shakti (creative power) and dissolves it through Samahara Sakthi (dissoutive power) Devi worship is, therefore the worship of God's glory, of his greatness and omnipotence. Devi is the conscious power of the Deva or God.

Sakthi is conceived of in its manifestation as Saraswathi, Laksmi and Kali which are not distinct Devis but the one formless Devi, worshipped in three different forms symbolising the creative, preservative and disolutive aspects of the Reality.

Thus Devi worship to an aspiring soul means the cultivation of knowledge and virtues and the destruction of the base nature. It creates one of the most beautiful relationships of the individual soul with the cosmic soul.

CHAPTER 13

Truthfulness by Tiruvallavur

If you should ask what truth maybe

Its a speech from every evil free If it will yield pure, unmixed good,

Truth may be replaced by falsehood

Do not lie about what your heart does know,

Such guilt will burn your heart aglow

If he lives true to his inner mind,

He lives in the heart of all mankind,

Greater he who speaks the truth with all his mind

Than those who do penance and charity combined,

No greater fame than words from falsehood free

Other virtues comes very easily

If truth and only truth, you speak

Other virtuous acts you need not seek

Outward cleanliness, the water will bestow

inner purity from truth will flow

All lamps are not lamps in wise men's sight

Truth is the only lamp with radiant light

Of all good things that we have learnt with care

Nothing can with truth compare

(excerpt from Tirukkural)

Thiruvalluver

There are a few Tamil literary compositions of a very early date which give us insight into the influence of the Dravidian civilisation in S India. The Thirukkural of Thiruvalluvar (one of the eighteen works collectively called the Keelkannakkul) is one of them. He was born in Madurai, and lived in Mylapore, Madras and was a weaver. His proper name is not known and the appellation refers to the Valluva caste (Pariahs or Harijans) to which he belonged. The first day of the Tamil month of Thai is accepted by Tamil scholars as his birthday. This ancient Tamil bard lived in the year 30 BC.

He is remembered for his 1330 exquisite couplets which are noted for wealth of wisdom, laconic brevity, lucidity and each expressing a profound truth. It is a code of ethics and morals applicable to people for all ages, and in respect of content and form without parallel. It propounds an ideal monarchy with ideal citizens who finally attain divine bliss. Tamil, one of the world's oldest living languages, was mature enough by 1st Century BC to produce a literary work hailed as the Tamil Veda. It's influence on the life of the people of Tamil Nadu can only be rivalled by the impact of the two national epics.

His verses have been translated into more than forty languages. The Hural teaches moral principles, discusses agriculture, statecraft, economics, military, science, medicine, education and the Law of Karma. It is divided into three parts.

Agam(ethics), Porrul (wealth) and its various disciplines and Inbam(enjoyment). These are regarded as the first three Purusathas that is objects which govern men's actions. As the last of the Purusarthas example: Moksha (liberation) is the final beatific and timeless state of the enfranchised soul and is not susceptible of approach through mere mental processes or literary effort, the great author-saint preferred to exclude it from the Kural.

Swami Sivananda

Kuppusamy was born on /9/1887 and was the son of Sri Vengu Lyer, a great Siva Bhakti and Shrimathi Parvathi Ammal. He was both intelligent and mischievous. At an early age he showed great love for his fellow human beings. He pitied the poor and fed the hungry including birds and animals.

At school he always topped the class and won prizes. After Matric he studied at a college in Thiruchirapalli. He participated in debates and dramas. After the completion of his first arts examination, he proceeded to medical school at Tanjore. He completed the MB, CM course and while practising at Thiruchi commenced a medical journal " The Ambrosia"

After the death of his father. He was called to Malaya to manage a hospital in a rubber estate. He was kind, sympathetic, humorous, witty and sweet speaking. People declared that he had a special gift from God for the miraculous cures he effected in his patients. In serious cases he kept vigil all night.

Despite his busy life, he served sadhus, sannyasis and beggars. A book given to him by a sadhu ignited the dormant spirituality in him. He studied the Gita, the Bhagavatam and the epics with great devotion. His immense philanthropy, spirit of service and renunciation endeared him to all. His heart was as pure as the Himalyan snow.

After renouncing the world in 1923, he left Malaya for India. He was initiated into the sanyasi's order by Swami Viswananda at Rishikesh and given the monastic name "Sivananda Saraswathi" He started the Divine Life Society in 1936 on the banks of the Holy Ganges for the propagation of the great culture and living idealism of India.

He radiated his divine and lofty messages of service, meditation, and God -Realisation to all parts of the world through his books. His devoted disciples are drawn from all religions, cults and creeds. He strove ceaselessly, to bring about a worldwide dissemination of the vital ethical and spiritual ideals and Dharma.

He had a natural flair for a life devoted to the study and practice of Vedanta. It was divine dispensation that he adopted a life of renunciation to minister to the soul of man. He lived and practised the Yoga of Synthesis and believed in the harmonious development of the human personality.

He preached the gospel of one humanity and the brotherhood of man. He propagated one caste (The caste of humanity), one religion (the religion of love), one commandment (the commandment of truthfulness) one law (the law of cause and effect) one God. (the omnipresent,omnipotent,and omniscient Lord) and one language (the language of the heart and silence)

He taught that the essentials of all religions are all the same, that differences only exist in the non-essentials and that every religion shows the correct path to God Realisation. He Attained Mahasamadhi on 14th July 1963

Bhagavan Sathiya Sai Baba

In 1872, itinerant Fakir settled in a deserted mosque in the village of Shirdi near Bombay. He was known as Sai Baba and performed astounding miracles and gave spiritual teachings to many Hindu,,Muslim and other devotees who gathered around him. His fame spread slowly due to poor communications. Before he died, he told one of his devotees , H.S..Dixit, a solicitor and Member of the Legislative Council of Bombay, that he would return as a boy in eighth years.

Exactly eight years later Satyanarayana was born of Telugu parentage in Puttaparthi, Andhra Pradesh on 23rd November 1926 to Pedda Raju and Easwaramma. Satya in Sanskrit means "Truth" or reality while Narayana is another appellation for Lord Vishnu. Before his birth, strange signs appeared in their home. For example: big tambours leaning against the wall would sometimes twang on its own in the middle of the night and the maddala (drum) on the floor would throb in the darkness as if an expert was beating it.

A priest told them that these events foretold an auspicious birth. Soon after his birth, the baby was placed on some bedclothes on the floor. After a while, the women in the room saw the clothes moving up and down and discovered that there was a cobra underneath. But the snake did not harm the child.

The presence of a cobra is somewhat significant as it is one of the symbols of Lord Siva. It is said the former Sai Baba of Shirdi, who died in 1918, appeared to the followers on occasions in the form of a cobra. Satyanarayana had a tender heart for all creatures. He was called Brahmujnani on account of his version for meat and his measure of love towards creation.

Puttaparthi is a hamlet that has carved out a niche for itself into the hearts of the people of the area, by legends that sanctify the memory and a history that inspired the young. The name is derived from "Putta" which means (anthill) in which a snake has taken up its abode and "Parthi" (a modified form of vardhini or multiplier).

Long ago the village was known as Gollapall (home of cowherds) for many years, the cows yielding copious milk until one day a cowherd was astonished when he discovered that his favourite cow had no milk in its udder when she returned from the hilly grazing grounds.

One day he followed the cow only to witness an even more astounding spectacle. A cobra emerged from the mound, raised itself and drank the milk. Enraged at the strange behaviour, he lifted a stone and heaved it on the cobra. Writhing in pain, the cobra threw a curse on the cowherd and foretold that the area would be full of anthills which would multiply endlessly. Soon the cattle declined in numbers and anthills spread all over and the name was changed to Valmikipuram or Puttaparthi in common parlance.

There is a temple in the village where the stone which is worshipped as Gopalaswami was installed some years ago. Sathiya Sai Baba revealed an interesting feature on this stone for when he requested some people to wash the stone and smear sandal paste, they could discern the clear outline of Sri Gopalaswami with his captivating flute and leaning on a cow.

Sai Baba began his formal education at the village school where he was an intelligent pupil. His special talents were drama, music, poetry and acting. At the age of eight, he wrote songs for the village opera.

Later he attended the higher elementary school at Bukkapatnam. He was in the habit of being early at school and, in the presence of other children, would conduct a worship (puja) using a holy image or picture and some flowers.

When he began attending high school at Uravakonda, he found that his fame had spread there before him. He was a fine writer and in Telugu, a good musician, a dancing exponent and was able to peep into the past and peep into the future. Soon he became the most popular figure at school and was the leader of the prayer group. He ascended the dias daily when the entire school assembled for prayers and his voice sanctified the air and inspired both teachers and taught to dedicate themselves to their duty.

Although it was his family's ambition that he should be educated for a good position as a government officer, strange events began to cast their shadows before them. One evening, in 1940, while walking barefooted, he leapt into the air with a loud shriek holding the toe of his right foot. His companions suspected it was a scorpion bitea although it was not. The next day, he fell unconscious leading to a stiff body and faint breathing.

The next day, when consciousness returned, he was by no means normal in behaviour. He had little interest in food, at times he would suddenly burst into song, sometimes quoted long Sanskrit passages far beyond what he had learnt at school, occasionally gave discourses on Vedanta Philosophy and describe far of places of pilgrimage which he had not visited.

Several doctors were consulted but were of no avail. Many thought that he was possessed by an evil spirit. On May 23 of that year, he assembled the members of the household and, with a wave of his hand, he produced sugar candy and flowers much to the amazement of those present. When his father appeared on the scene and asked him whether he was a God, a madcap or a ghost, he answered calmly and firmly. "I am Sai Baba". Not many people had heard of this name before.

Thursday is regarded as Guru's day in India and on this day every week, people gathered around their new Guru, Satyanarayana. At one of these sessions, someone asked, " If you are really Sai Baba, show us a sign". He then requested for some jasmine flowers to be placed in his hand and with a quick gesture threw them on the floor. All those present looked in awe as the flowers had fallen to form the name " Sai Baba" in Telugu script. The words were strikingly clear as if arranged with meticulous skill and all the curves and convolutions of the letters were perfectly produced.

Perhaps the most interesting phenomenon was the regular production of ash (vibuthi) Although he returned to college after a lapse of six months, the final break from the studies came on October 20 when he decided to throw away his books and announced that he was leaving. At this moment , a halo appeared around his head which almost blinded those near him.

Although he was not anxious to return home, pleas from his parents resulted in his return to Puttaparthi. Throughout the years since he made the astonishing claim that he was the reincarnation of India's most mysterious and powerful modern saint, Shirdi Baba, there has been much evidence to support this claim.

The underlying theme of these teachings is that we must seek God through self-surrender and devotion. The soul, which had completely surrendered itself, blotting out the lower ego , is able to absorb and gain all the benefits from the silent teaching which the Sadguru radiates. His spiritual guidance differs for each individual disciple, for it depends on one's temperament, state of progress and needs at the time.

He strives constantly to show the basic unity between all religions. Among his devoted disciples are people of all leading faiths. This is the greatness of the Sanathana Dharma, the eternal spiritual law - this insistence on the oneness behind the apparent multiplicity. The atma which it declares to be the basic truth, does not contradict the doctrines of any faith. God is unlimited by space and time. He is indefinable by names or forms.

The spiritual guidance given by Sai Baba to spiritual aspirants is the Bhakti way embodied in the following principles:-

The aspirant must realise the triviality of the things of this world.

He must realise that he is in bondage to the lower worlds and as an intense desire to be free.

Our senses have been created to move outwards. To attain self-realisation and an immortal life, we must turn our gaze inwards and look to the inner self.

One must refrain from wrongdoing to attain self realisation.

A life of truth, penance, insight and right conduct is essential.

Always choose the good instead of the pleasant.

The aspirant must control his mind and senses.

Purify the mind and get rid of avarice and egoism.

All aspirants must have a Guru.

The most important thing is to obtain the Lord's Grace.

Sai Baba expounded the Perennial Philosophy or Ancient Wisdom that is :

This ever-changing world is a changeless eternal Reality. Philosophers call it the Absolute and Hindus term it Brahman. Like the circumference of a circle, which it uses as its symbol , it has no beginning and no end. Brahman is a changeless background against a constantly changing universe.

The second concept is that man's Spirit called the "Athman" or "Self" is identical with Brahman. It is possible for a human being to reach his Athman and to identify himself with his Spirit. This can only be done by means of the third concept.

The aim of Man's life on earth is to discover his true identity. His earthly life is not his main purpose but this can be used as a means to reach his goal that is from ignorance to Knowledge , from darkness to Light and from the transient to the Eternal.

In order to realise one's divine identity, one must travel the road of Yoga. This road, like a modern expressway, has a number of lanes of which one is best suited to one's psycho-physical vehicle in which one is travelling. Few can travel, on the fast lane of Jnana Yoga, without a particular kind of mental constitution, and is not meant for those in the preliminary stages of spiritual development.

It is difficult to make steady progress on any lane of the Yoga highway with Divine inspiration which comes through the emergence, from time to time, of Divine Incarnation in human form. Intense love and devotion to any God-man is called the Bhakti Marga or the Yoga of Devotion. This loving worship of an incarnation and constant contemplation of his attributes offers the easiest course for the majority of people.

Whatever the pathway selected , the important thing to remember is that man has a double nature , a false ego created by his desires and an eternal Self. His yogic task is to eradicate this false ego with Divine Light and so merge it into his eternal Self.

The macro cosmos and the Microcosmos - the Brahmanda and the Pindanda- the Universal and the individual-all arise from the one Truth. They are manifestations and emergents of that one Truth which is not affected by either. That Truth is known as Brahman.

The basic Truth upon which Maya (illusion) projects its kaleidoscope is described by seers as Sath-Chith-Ananda. This does not mean that Brahman has three attributes or characteristics, that is - exists beyond time and space; it knows and can be known; it is the source and acme of bliss.

Maya is the only Divine Will that inaugurated the manifestation of the Cosmos. It has three aspects of achievement through the three modes and moods of that Will, that is the Sathwic (the calm, contented, equanimous mood); the rajasic (the potent, passionate mood) and the thamasic (the inert, slothful, sluggish mood). The facets of that Will are called jnana sakthi, icca sakthi and kriya shakti.

These three modes affect beings and things in various proportions and permutations and so we have all the variety and diversity of an objective world. Maya is a clear flawless mirror. When the sathwik nature is reflected in that mirror, God results, when the rajasic nature is reflected, the jiva or individualised self results and when the tamasic nature is reflected, matter (the objective world) results.

The headquarters of the Sai Foundation is at Puttaparthi and is known as Prasanthi Nilayam or the Abode of Tranquility which was inaugurated on 23rd November 1950, the twenty-fifth birthday of Sathya Sai Baba. He was the architect and engineer who directed the entire work of construction.

CHAPTER 14

Prayer And Festivals

Pongal is a harvest festival of thanksgiving. It is the most important and most widely celebrated festival in S India. It falls on the first day in the Tamil month of Thai when the sun enters its northern course towards the Tropic of Capricorn, hence it is also known as Makara Sankaranthi.

It is considered to be Dravidian in origin and dates back to 2000BC when the Indus Valley was inhabited by the Dravidians. These people were mainly farmers and depended on Mother Earth, personified as Goddess Laksumi, for their livelihood. The symbolism of Pongal is an expression of thanksgiving to the forces of nature for the bounteous harvest. It is a four day cultural festival.

Surya Pongal

This marks the main ceremony and is dedicated to the Sun (Surya), the farmers greatest benefactor and the primary source of energy. Fresh produce (pumpkins, sugar cane, sweet potatoes) are gathered from the fields and spread out ceremoniously before the rising sun.

A fireplace is built and fuel is supplied by freshly cut palmyra leaves. A new clay pot is embellished with red powder (Kumkum or saffron) and holy ash, Turmeric and ginger plants are tied around the pot by means of threads. The pot is then placed on the fire and filled with milk and water. As the milk boils, some newly harvested rice is put into the pot . When the rice boils, spices are added. As the milk boils over, everyone cries: " Pongolo, Pongal, Pongolo,Pongal" (Hail Pongal)

Thai Poosam

This festival falls during the month of Thai and the most famous places where it is observed are at Palani and Thiruthani in South India, where thousands of people are worshippers of Lord Muruga. The festival falls on a new moon day. Kavadies are decorated with marigolds and peacock feathers and brass vessels, containing milk are tied to the ends of the kavadies.

Some devotees fall into a trance as if controlled by some hypnotic power. Other devotees have their tongues pierced with silver needles, representing Lord Subramanya's lance (vel) Some have lime fruit hooked on to their bodies by means of silver hooks, while some even draw a chariot. The subjection to rigorous austerities rids oneself of the ego, anger and lust. At intervals, attendants pour rose water on the tongues pierced and turmeric water on the feet of devotees.

Although kavadi processions are designed to follow distances of several miles, in our country, the tendency is to follow a route that circumambulated the temple. Lord Muruga is believed to be endowed with power to destroy all ills. Piercing the body with needles or walking on burning coals are regarded as acts of atonement to win the Grace of Lord Muruga, who grants the boon of liberation to all who worship him with unflinching devotion.

Sivarathri

While Navarathri is dedicated to the various aspects of Bakthi, Sivarathri is dedicated to Lord Siva who reveals himself in many different and often contradictory forms, one of the most important being Lord of the Dance. According to the Tamil Calender, Siarathri is of five types. That is Paksha which occurs fortnight; Mass which occurs monthly; Yoga is the night which a Yogi creates for himself by his Yogic trance;Nitya (daily night of Siva) and Maha Sivarathri which occurs annually,,in the month of Masi, on the fourteenth lunar day as Saturthasi in the waning fortnight of the moon that is the day preceding the new moon.

The festival is meticulously observed at all Siva temples and homes by devoted Hindus belonging to both the Vaishnavite and Saivite sects. A period of fasting is supposed to precede the day . The night which is divided into four quarters known as Yamums is spent in a devotional atmosphere. Prayers are conducted with appropriate rites during each of the Yamums, hence Lord Siva is worshipped in four different ways during the night.

The image of Lord Siva is anointed with milk, curd, clarified butter and honey, respectively, during the Yamums as follows:

1st Yamum Lord Siva is worshipped with lotus flowers, a preparation called pongal (rice and dal mixed) is offered and the Rig Veda is recited.

2nd Yamum worship with Tulsi leaves, offer payasam (sweet preparation) and recite from Yajur Veda

3rd Yamum worship with leaves of Bael tree called Bilvam in Tamil, offer food mixed with sesame powder and recite from Sama Veda

4th Yamum worship with Blue Lotus, offer simple food and recite from the Athavana Veda.

Purattasi

This month is a period of continuous worship for a large segment of the S Indians who propiste Lord Venketeswara (Venketas Perumal) the presiding deity of the Tirupati Temple in Andhra Pradesh. It is time to exercise considerable discipline . Although it is an important occasion for Vaishnavite Hindus of the S Indian origin, many Saivites also observe the festival.

The festival of Lord Venkateswara is held annually on the Tirumala Hills. The famous Tirupati Temple, which is considered the richest in India, lies in Andhra Pradesh and attracts millions of pilgrims. Although a variety of offerings are made, the characteristic offering is shaving of the hair from one's head. The Sanskrit University of Thirupathi is maintained from the income received by this temple.

During this month, people restrict themselves to a vegetarian diet and abstain from all vices. Some homes are so scrupulously clean that even a new set of cooking utensils are used. Many fast on Saturdays and abstain from eating or drinking water until the afternoon when the fast is broken after prayer.

On one Saturday during the month, a special prayer is conducted . Before this, all male members of the household have a Vaishnavite sign called " Naamam" painted on their foreheads. The sign is made of two vertical white strokes joined together at the bottom with a red vertical stroke in the centre.

These white strokes represent the pair of sandals belonging to Rama handed to Bharat at the time of Rama's banishment. This special prayer is commenced outside and after worshipping the Sun, the entire household members enter the home lighting camphor in clay lamps and uttering, " Govinda, Govinda" Appropriate hymns are sung.

This festival appears to have been introduced into Tamil Nadu by the Mysore Kings who were once overlords of some of the Tamil areas.In Mysore, it is celebrated as Dasara Festival. The correct significance of the festival is shrouded in mystery. According to mythology, it was during this month that Lord Vishnu killed Hiranya who believed that he was omnipotent God and ordered everyone to worship him.

Deepavali, the festival of lights, symbolises the conquest of evil by the forces of good and righteousness. It is the triumph of light over darkness and victory of virtue over vice.On this day, we pray so that Almighty will give us faith,hope and courage to spread the common gospel of all religions - the brotherhood of man.

The name originates from two Sanskrit words that are deepam, deepa, or deepak (light) and avall (a row) or oil(rays of radiance of the lamp.)It is celebrated in the month of Aypassi, at the end of the 14th lunar day known as Sathurthi, in the waning fortnight of the moon with all its sanctity, splendour,colour,grandeur and festivity. Although the mythological theme behind it varies in different parts of the country , the underlying theme is always the same.

It is an occasion which brings brilliance and rays of hope and inspiration unshakably as a beacon to all. The festival is identified with the religio-cultural life of the Hindu community. Various interpretations have been given from age to age with regard to its origin. Some of these have historical association, while others are of mythological significance. In its ultimate analysis, it represents a symbol of the climax of Hindu spiritual aspirations.

Defined in its philosophical context, the historical-mythological explanations of this festival are but oversimplification of deep spiritual truths. In this material world, life for the Hindus is a conflict between "Light" and " Darkness" and between " Good" and "Evil". The former makes for release from births and deaths resulting in eternal union with the Absolute , while the latter confines us to bondage in the world of suffering.

CHAPTER 15

Origin of Tamil

Tamil belongs to the Pancha Dravida that is a group of 5 Dravidian Languages that is Tamil, Telugu, Kannada, Malayalam and Tulu. The generally accepted view of its origin is that Agastya, the disciple of Lord Siva, studied the language under his guru and proceeded to S India where he established an ashram in the caves of Podiya Malal.

Madurai symbolises the oldest centre of Tamil learning and the Chola and Pandyan Kings were its patrons. It has its panini in Tholkappiar, Vedic Rishi in Agastya, Upanishadic Sage in Thiruvalluvar and Vainaki in Kamar.

Tamil is an original classical language of qualified grace and opulent melody. It is a repertory and storehouse of devotional hymns. It's grammar, diction and prosody are distinctively original. The erosive ocean inundations swallowed up most of the land and with it most of its precious literary treasures . The most ancient work Tholkappiam which is the authoritative Tamil grammar and rhetoric existed 9000 years ago. It contains details on alphabet,words, pronunciation and syntax. It is divided into nine sections . This masterpiece of grammar contains 1612 verses.

Tamil is a classical language like Sanskrit and Latin and has 30 alphabets (twelve vowels and eighteen consonants) representing different sounds.

History of the Gounders (Govender)

One theory derives it from the Tamil word *Kaamindan*, meaning "noble protector of the country", later modified as *Kavundan* or Gounder.were rulers of many dynasties such as Velir,Durvinita of the Ganga dynasty.

Gounders were originally ancient brave warriors(Kshatriya) and later farmed and raised cattle in the Kongu region. Gounders were most of the Zamindars and other Chieftains. Gounders were included as forward caste during independence and later changed to Below caste as requested. Gounders also developed in Singapore(Singa Pura) and Cambodia. Gounders had an identity of being great landlords. There are also agricultural labourers among the Gounder community. Since the arrival of textile mills many have found work as labourers in these industries. During the late 1800s many gounders went to work in South African Sugarcane farms as indentured labourers.

Great grandfather Ellappa was of the Vanniyar caste.

Hiltebeitel, who classifies the Vanniyar as Shudra in the Hinduvarna system, notes that South Indian society traditionally recognised neither the Kshatriya (warrior) norVaishya (provider) varnas, being divided instead between Brahmins on the one hand and Shudras and untouchables on the other. Nonetheless, communities in the region frequently sought to prove a historic higher status, based on myth or occasionally probable history. He notes that "traditions of demotion from a once higher rank are a commonplace of South Indian caste mythologies Researcher Lloyd I Rudolf notes that as early as in 1833, the Vanniyar, who were then known as Pallis, had ceased to accept their "low caste" status, also described as being Shudra by Christophe Jaffrelot and Kathleen Gough and Gough, however, documenting her fieldwork of 1951-53, records the Palli and the Vanniyar as separate but similar cultivating castes

The majority of those who arrived in the country could neither read nor write but had some knowledge of the treasure house of their religion, culture and traditions. They had learnt much of their religion by word of mouth and they passed this on to their children in the same oral tradition. They also brought with them the caste system, their religious practises, rituals and dogmas, kept them alive and handed them down to succeeding generations. There were some mendicant bards who were literate and knew portions of the great epics.

The manner and the circumstances of their departure from their native land and the condition in which they arrived in this country, has had a tremendous impact on their future lives. The immigrant labourers were violently torn from their traditional moorings and transported to a foreign country in such a manner that they lost all contact with their own kith and kin and were eager to develop new ties. These circumstances made them less conservative and more susceptible to changes in their customs, habits and language.

The Tamil people were drawn from the state of Madras - the districts of Salem, Kumbakonam, Tirunelveli, Trichy, Chidambaram, Tanjore, Madurai, and Chingleput

Philosophy

The world was conceived as a unity of reality, manifesting itself in many different appearances. Religion was seen as a unity of Truth expressing itself in many different creeds. Both Truth and Reality are understood as manifestations of the pervasive principle of unity in diversity. This tolerant, synthetic and synoptic spirit of ancient Indian thought has given to her culture, throughout the ages, resilience and flexibility which have enabled it to permeate the entire mass of the people and resists all attempts to break the continuity and the life of the ancient tradition.

The process of synthesis continues to this day. Tagore sang of it in his magnificent ode that has become India's National Anthem, and Gandhi expressed it in his reverence of all faiths. In this capacity for reconciliation, renewal and growth lies the secret of the unity, the continuity and the richness of the culture of India.

The tamilakam or the ancient home of the Tamils was regarded as the cradle of the human race. Although other civilisations rose and perished, the Tamils remained stable despite an onslaught by invaders and conquerors. Strange to say that it was the foreigners who discovered the ancient Tamil language.

The ancient Tamils were ruled by kings, wrote alphabetical characters on palmyra leaves, had laws and customs and were occupied in spinning, weaving and dvelna. They believed in the existence of God (Ko) and their temples were called (Koil). They had a well-ordered social harmony, efficient government, and richness of art as is evident from the works of Thirukkural (the Aphorisms of Saint Valluvar).

The Sangam Age

During this period, the Chera, Chola and Pandiyan kingdoms flourished in Tamil Nadu. Hereditary monarchy existed and the king was commander-in-chief of the army which consisted of the chariotry, elephantry, cavalry and infantry. As people expected him to be a model ruler, he set a high standard in following ethical codes. Poetry, music and dancing flourished under the patronage of the kings while hunting, wrestling, boxing and dice-play were popular sports.

The Pallava Period

Many of the Pallava rulers were versatile and gifted kings.- dramatists, musicians, builders, theologians and warriors. They contributed much to the development of religion, literature, art and music. This period witnessed the revival of both Saivism and Vaishnavism. They encouraged the building of a number of temples. The Pallava era of South India's history represents a transition from the ancient to the medieval. Mahendra Varman was the first Pallava ruler to excavate temples from solid rocks and Kancheepuram was the capital.

His son, Narishimha Varna, was a great builder of rock temples example: Mahabalipuram.

The Cheras

They ruled the west coast and had substantial foreign trade in ivory and spices.

The Chola Period

This dynasty consisted of men and women who had, as their heritage, aesthetic appreciation, intellectual curiosity and religious devotion. They are specifically remembered for their great work in temple buildings. In the casting of bronze idols, their craftsmanship was unique.

They revitalised the village administration by making the officials assume great powers and responsibilities. They paid attention to water resources by digging up lakes and constructing dams. Some of these are standing monuments to their engineering skill. They are noted for their immediate redressal of public grievances, for example, they hung the Araichi-mani (call bell) which anyone could ring in an emergency to interview the king.

Later Chola Period

This was a magnificent and glorious age in the history of Tamilakam. King Vijaya revived the Chola dynasty and captured Tanjore from the Pallavas. They ruled from the 9th-12th century AD. King Raja Raja 1 (985 -1014) extended his rule to Kerala, Mysore and Ceylon. He built the magnificent temple of Rajarajeswaram (the finest specimen of Tamil architecture) at Tanjore. He carved with gold, the sanctum sanctorum of the Chidambaram temple.

Although an ardent adherent of Lord Siva, he showed tolerance to all other sects and religions. King Rajendra 1 (1014-1044) who succeeded his father, sent a mighty expedition to Kadaram (Malay Peninsula) where he brought under his rule several cities and islands. This demonstrates the great naval strength of the Cholas.

They established an admirable administrative system in the country with the King as the supreme head of the executive judiciary, army, navy and the entire civil administration. The temple served as the hub of the community and was used for worship, philosophical discussions, entertainment, festivals, music and dancing.

The Pandyan Period

Their sphere of influence was in the extreme south. They rendered signal service to the development of Tamil literature. Jayavarman Sundara Pandya (1211-1270) was the most famous Pandyan King. After conquering the Cholas, he ruled for 20 years from Madurai to Ceylon. The quarrels between his two sons, Vira Pandya and Sundra Pandya, paved the way for a Moslem invasion which was thwarted by the rise of the Vijayanagar kingdom which ruled the country during the 14th century AD.

Buddha - Jain Period

At the end of the Sangam period, Buddhism and Jainism began to extend their influence into Tamil Nadu. The period subsequent to 200BC saw the dawn of the era of the Jain-Buddhist cult. Prior to this, the only religious cult was Saivism.

The Salva Period

Buddhism and Jainism flourished until 500 AD. Both gained a considerable foothold but failed to give peace and spiritual bliss to the people and Saivism once more established itself firmly in Tamil Nadu.

Vijayanagar Nayak Period

The Vijayanagar rule, for the period of 150 years, was supervised by the Viceroys and later by the Nayaks. Visvanatha (1529-1564) introduced the Palayam system by dividing his kingdom into 72 palayams. (districts) and placed each one under a chieftain called Palayagar. Some of the queens who ruled during this time were Meenakshi and Mangammal.

The Vijayanagar kings enlarged the scope and contents of the festivals and introduced halls with thousands of pillars. They encouraged the large-scale migration of Brahmins and craftsmen from Andhra Pradesh to Tamil Nadu.

Spiritual Death

This term may be slightly off-putting, but it isn't meant to suggest physical death. What 'dies' are all our illusions and delusions about who we are and how things really are. This is usually spoken of as 'insight practice' (*vipassana*). Insight can be cultivated through a huge range of meditation, mindfulness, and awareness practices. All of those already mentioned have insight dimensions. Others widely practiced in the Triratna Buddhist Community and Order include reflections on the three *lakshanas* ('Characteristics', or 'Marks') of conditioned existence.

The first, impermanence, involves contemplating the transitoriness of all composite things. Then comes contemplation of unsatisfactoriness: reflecting that seeking security or meaning for our lives in such transitory things will inevitably lead to being let down and consequent suffering. Finally, reflection on insubstantiality involves contemplating that there is no ultimately existing, graspable 'essence' in anything. Contemplations such as this can lead to a loosening of the human tendency to grasp onto life and opening up to the ultimate mystery of our true nature.

The third stage, of Spiritual Death, is not of course the end of the process. After you have been integrated, made your mind positive and refined, and 'died' spiritually, the question arises – 'What is there? What is left? What comes into being?'. What comes into being, in Sangharashita's system of meditation, is a new being, the new you – a new being based not on selfishness, but on wisdom and compassion. That new being is the *Bodhisattva*. So the meditator is reborn (not literally, of course, but metaphorically) as a Bodhisattva. He or she becomes something quite new, quite different. Instead of being driven by ego, it is the Bodhicitta that comes through you: this is the stage of spiritual rebirth.

ACKNOWLEDGEMENTS

This book would not have been made possible without the help of others.

First and foremost credit must be given to my dear husband and children for their undivided loyalty, patience, and understanding in my need for privacy and personal space.

To all the patients, residents and friends whom I have met and worked with, it is a privilege and honour to serve you. For 30 odd years, I have learned patience, tolerance, empathy and understanding from you. I learned to laugh and find joy in the simple things in life.

To my best Friends

Thank you for accepting me for who I am, though my faults, you accept me. You show me the way of life. You are loving, caring, supportive, and kind. I would be lost without you in my life.

The following publications have been helpful in my research during the course of writing this book :

A documentary history of the Indian South Africans

The Imperial Gazetteer of India

Essays on Indentured Indians in Natal

Our Glorious Heritage

The Gandhi org

Wikipedia

Himalaya Academy

Printed in Great Britain
by Amazon